duolingo
english test

ESSENTIAL TIPS, STRATEGIES, PRACTICE, GRAMMAR & VOCABULARY TO SCORE 125+

ASHOK MUNJAL
MASTER TRAINER

ENGLISH WORLD
KURUKSHETRA

INDEX

ACKNOWLEDGEMENT

Blessed are those who have the blessings of God, the company of helping and considerate family members, friends and well-wishers. In this regard, I perceive that I am blessed more than what I deserve.

While writing these contents, my family members always supported me, and helped me complete this project by sparing me from the mundane routine of life. I clearly understand that this project would not have seen the daylight if they had not cooperated.

The name of Mr. Ranjan Sharma always comes first in my mind when I think of acknowledging someone as he is the one who has always motivated me in this journey

My esteemed associates and close friends have always been an inspiring force to write these contents. Especially Mr. Ajay Mandhara, Mr. Sukhbeer, Ms. Apsara and Ms. Seema Rani have always encouraged me a lot to complete the contents. Their contributions cannot be reciprocated in any way through this acknowledgment.

I have been in the profession of teaching the English language for more than 15 years. During my teaching experience, I learned a lot from my students who came from different walks of life with different levels of knowledge. I acknowledge their contribution in making me an established English Trainer.

Last but not least, a ton of thanks to various applications and websites like duolingo.com, vocabulary.com, wes.org, magoosh.com englishclub.com, preply.com ieltsbuddy.com, ielts-blog.com, gingersoftware.com, fluent.com, ieltsexampreparation.com, whichhave enriched my knowledge.

Thanks to one and all, who have not been mentioned, but I understand their indirect contribution in completing these contents.

ASHOK MUNJAL

MASTER TRAINER (ENGLISH WORLD KURUKSHETRA)

Helpline-94168-21236

MESSAGE FROM AUTHOR

When you are preparing for your Duolingo English test or any other English exam, you know how difficult it is to score well in these exams.

This Duolingo English test preparation material is not like traditional resources. It has been prepared after observing the various issues of the test and concerns of the common students.

Since the Duolingo English test is American, most of the spellings used in this book are American. Specifically, spellings like color, traveling, organization, recognize, center, liter, meter, empathize, analyze, program, generalize, socialize may create doubts among Indian students as they are used to reading and learning the U.K.'s spellings. Another doubtful area can be a comma before 'and' and 'or'. In this book, the U.K.'s compounding (Conjunctions) rules have been followed. Hence, students are advised to use their wisdom before thinking anything else.

In the actual test, both types of spellings and grammar rules are accepted.

It is hopefully believed that learners of all the levels will find the contents of this book worth reading.

All the best to the students appearing for Duolingo English test for their endeavors.

What is the Duolingo English Test?

The Duolingo English Test is an online English language examination that you take on your personal computer from the comforts of your home. Like the PTE, TOEFL and IELTS, it tests all four language skills: Reading, Listening, Speaking, and Writing. However, you'll find these skills tested in pretty revolutionary ways!

The test is adaptive which means, it has some significant consequences for test-takers. If you answer a question correctly, the next one gets harder. If your answer is wrong, the next one gets easier. This means that with relatively a few questions, the exam can pinpoint your ability level quickly—that's why it only takes around an hour to complete.

Why should you take the Duolingo English Test?

Duolingo is primarily being accepted in Canada and the U.S. for undergraduate admissions. Moreover, Duolingo could be a good option for you if you don't do well in traditional English exams like PTE, TOEFL or IELTS. The format is completely different, and maybe easier for you.

How is the Duolingo English Test different from the IELTS/PTE/TOEFL?

Though all the tests can be computer-based, there are many differences between the Duolingo exam and the IELTS/PTE/TOEFL. Those differences go far beyond the location, timing, and price!

The first thing you'll notice is that Duolingo test items look different from traditional test items. There aren't long texts to read, listen to, or write about. Most of the items on the Duolingo exam are relatively brief; Besides, IELTS/PTE/TOEFL divides question type by section (Reading, Listening, Speaking, and Writing), while Duolingo blends all questions into a single exam. You may encounter a reading question followed by a writing question. This can require the test takers to think on their feet and change the gears pretty quickly.

How long is the test?

Somewhere between 55 and 60 minutes; however, to some extent, it depends on your English level. Since the test is adaptive, a proficient test-taker can finish the test in a shorter period.

How should you prepare for the Duolingo English Test?

It's tricky to prepare for the Duolingo exam as it measures everything from how natural your intonation is to your ability to accurately describe a photo you've never seen before! However, there are a few things you can do to ensure you're ready to take it. The best thing you can do for your score on the Duolingo exam is to work on your overall English proficiency using high-level materials including this reference and practice book. Further, you should read well-written articles, listen to podcasts in English, understand the rules of grammar, learn new words, get acquainted with spellings of typical words and have as many conversations as you can with English speakers.

Since the Duolingo English test presents you with unusual item types, it's really important to take the short (8-10-minutes) practice test on the Duolingo official website. The sample test is a great opportunity to understand how the test interface works.

Understand the rules

The rules include not wearing earphones, not interacting with anyone else, not using your phone or other devices, and not looking off-screen. It is important to follow these rules during the test, or you will need to take it again. Since you take the Duolingo English Test online from your computer, you will have to make sure that you have everything you need to avoid encountering any tribulation while taking the test. Ultimately you must have:

- A government-issued photo ID

- A quiet, well-lit room

- About one hour of uninterrupted time

- A computer equipped with a front-facing camera

- An internet connection and a compatible browser
  Duolingo has some stringent rules in place to make sure that you're the one taking the test—without any additional help.

You'll be required to be alone and nobody else can be in the room with you or speak to you during the exam. You can't turn away from the browser window for the length of the test (it may be helpful to go into the full-screen mode to prevent this!). You have to show your ears for the entire test, so get an elastic band ready if your hair is long. There are other guidelines to follow, so make sure you read them through before sitting for the exam.

What may be most difficult for those used to other exams is that you can't take any notes. Since the exam questions are relatively short, you don't need to take notes during it. However, if you're a life-long note-taker, this can be a hard habit to break! This is another area where taking the practice test can get you ready for the full experience.

What happens after you take the Duolingo English Test?

After you complete the exam, it's sent to the proctors, and you'll receive an email letting you know when you'll get your scores (48 hours). When your scores are ready, you'll get another email notifying you, though you'll also be able to check into your home page on the site to check.

You can take two "certified" tests within 30 days. A certified test is any test you complete and receive a score on. In other words, if you have technical glitches during the exam, it won't count against the two-test limit. Scores are then valid for two years.

Once your scores are in, you can send them to institutions right from the results page. There's no limit to how many reports you can send.

Is the Duolingo English proficiency test right for you?

If you're applying to colleges in Canada or the U.S. which accept it - it could be a good choice; however, you should check in advance with the university or college to which you want to apply, whether it accepts it or not as a proof of your English level requirements.

How is the test scored?

Once the exam is over, you'll receive a score from 10-160. This is a holistic score, not broken down by section. Top programs may require a score above 120, but requirements differ, so check with each school/college/university. You can also see how your score on Duolingo roughly correlates to IELTS scores.

Duolingo	IELTS
75-80	5
85-90	5.5
95-100	6
105-110	6.5
115-120	7
125-130	7.5
130-140	8
145-150	8.5
155-160	9

<u>What does the test Involve?</u>

You'll see a variety of test items on Duolingo in formats that may be entirely new to you. The test includes:

- Typing a statement that you hear
- Completing missing letters from a text
- Listening to spoken words and selecting the real ones
- Reviewing written words and selecting the real ones
- Describing an image in writing or aloud
- Recording yourself saying a written sentence
- Verbally answering a spoken question
- Responding in writing to a written question in 50 words

In addition to the above items, Duolingo includes a "video interview" section of the exam, in which you speak for 1-3 minutes on a topic you choose (they offer two), and write on a chosen topic out of two topics for 3-5 minutes. These two activities are ungraded, but go along with your test results to universities/colleges—which can be a great addition to your application!

Different tasks of Duolingo English Test

During the test, you will be asked to complete various tasks (11-12) that test your speaking, reading, listening and writing skills. You can expect tasks such as:

Task-1(30 Seconds for each statement)
Maximum no. of statements- 5

Type the statement that you hear – This is a simple task of writing what you hear with the option to repeat the audio 3 times. Here you are being tested on your listening comprehension, vocabulary, spelling and punctuations' skills.

Tip! The accents that you hear are American, if you're not familiar with this accent then start watching American TV and film or listening to an American podcast.

Type the statement that you hear

Nobody has ever mentioned it.

Number of replays left: 2

Sample Statements

Try to type these statements mentioned below after asking somebody to speak

o The most striking thing about this budget cannot be seen.
o Many students are so scared of writing essays.
o People with an active lifestyle are less likely to die early.
o Eating too much can lead to many health problems
o The author is currently the Professor at Cambridge University.
o Biographic information should be removed.
o Our logbooks make up five percent of the total marks.
o You may need to purchase an academic gown.
o Good research delivers practical benefits.

Task-2(60 Seconds for each list)
Maximum no. of lists- 3

Choose the real words from a written list - In this task, you are given a list of words up to 18, some are real and some are made up(fake), and you are asked to choose only the correct ones.

Tip! Be careful with choosing the correct word and make sure you check the spelling as some words look as they might be correct, but in fact, are made up! The words in green color are the real words.

enviorenment	strict	pertinent	**bonjoir**	**temprature**
standard	**brouser**	mellodrama	Creature	stringent
literature	**discipnile**	**sliggish**	**ostinate**	lukewarm

List-1

pharmceutical	**vovacious**	ravishing	filthy	licentious
garnish	sedentary	dare	brighten	**lirtery**
circality	grandeur	**girigarous**	derogatory	chide

List -2

aberration	**paragone**	**Parabigm**	Example	Rap
inflation	swamped	Repercussion	Reaction	Specious
sedentary	Denounce	**Enticen**	**Temtious**	Profound

List -3

Diligent	Throttle	**Severence**	Rigid	Filthy
Wilt	**Collassp**	**Modishen**	**Stylis**	Nostaelgic
Indolent	Lazy	Restoration	**Restablish**	Over

List -4

Task-3(3 Minutes for each paragraph)
Maximum no. of paragraphs- 3

Complete the words in a paragraph – This task requires you to complete the missing letters in selected words in a given paragraph. You're being tested on vocabulary knowledge, sentence formation and grammar structures.

You should try revising some specific spellings, vocabulary and dependent prepositions to help prepare for this part of the test, and in case you get stuck on any particular word, read the line again and find out the context in which the sentence of the paragraph is written. Besides, complete the exercises mentioned below to have firsthand experience, and read the spelling and vocabulary sections of this book (in red color) from page number 52 to 62 to increase your base of understanding the different types of words which you may encounter in this task.

1 Over-packaging of produ_ _ _ has become a trend in this compete_ _ _ _ world. Producers are trying to attract consu_ _ _ _ with an attractive packaging of their products, not bother_ _ _ about its negative impact not only on our environ_ _ _ _ but also on the users. It should be the respons_ _ _ _ _ _ _ of the producers to limit the wastage of the resources in the form of unnecess_ _ _ packaging.

2 The cost of over packaging is actually add_ _ to the product sold. In fact, It is seen that the packing cost and durability is more than the prod_ _ _ itself. The type of packaging found in pharmaceuti_ _ _ industries can be taken as an example here. Pills and tab_ _ _ _ are found to be packed in much bigger and colour_ _ _ strips thanneeded. Does this increase the sale of medi_ _ _ _ ?

3 Success in any area of life never happens in a compl_ _ _ vacuum. It is just dependent on an individual's will-power, intellig_ _ _ _ ,environ_ _ _ _ and outside circumst_ _ _ _ _ . To find happiness and success, one, therefore, needs to pay atten_ _ _ _ and take some control over the type of environments one is surrounded on the daily ba_ _ _.

4 The frequent rise in temper_ _ _ _ _ due to global warming has adversely affected the entire crea_ _ _ _ on this Earth. No one is left from the wor_ _ _ impact of this cli_ _ _ _ change. Concerted efforts by all individuals, Government and organization are needed to save the sanc_ _ _ _ of nature.

5 TV, news_ _ _ _ _ and radios play an import_ _ _ role in people's lives. it is possi_ _ _ to claim that newspapers, mass media and radio update us what is going on in this wor_ _ , and also all these sources help people raise their stand_ _ _ of lives. There are several reasons why newspapers, TV and radio are consider_ _ to be Advantage_ _ _ _ to us.

6 Actively engaging workers in the decision-making proc_ _ _ increases overall company mor_ _ _ . Employees understand their ideas and knowledge. They provide an important contri_ _ _ _ _ _ to the company, and give them the power to influence the outcome of their work leading to increas_ _ job satisfaction and a positive attitude. Using employees in the decision-making process, rather than outsour_ _ _ _ , saves money and time.

7 For higher studies, some people travel abroad even th_ _ _ _ we have great doctor_ _ _ _ who completed their research stud_ _ _ without moving from away from their hometowns. Truly speaking, we are not require_ _ to move to other count_ _ _ _ for higher educa_ _ _ _ .

8 Some of the stud_ _ _ _ and parents have their mindset that migration for
Post graduat_ _ _ and under graduation would be benefit_ _ . They assume that the qua_ _ _ _ of univers_ _ _ _ _ in their country is not sophisti_ _ _ _ _ for the students' future, however, at that same time, the stud_ _ _ who belong to mid_ _ _ class, they are never tau_ _ _ that they would go to another country for university studies.

9 This task requi_ _ _ you to compl_ _ _ the missing letters in select_ _ words in a given para_ _ _ _ _ . You're being tested on vocabu_ _ _ _ knowledge, sent_ _ _ _ formation and grammar structu_ _ _ .

10 Just beca_ _ _ you're at home, it doesn't mean that rule_ go out of the wind_ _! In fact, Duo_ _ _ _ _ test has some strin_ _ _ _ rules in place to make sure that you're the one tak_ _ _ the test—without any addition_ _ help.

ANSWERS:

1. Products, Competitive, Consumers, Bothering, Environment, Responsibility, Unnecessary

2. Adding, Product, Pharmaceutical, Tablets, Colourful, Medicine

3. Complete, Intelligence, Environment, Circumstances, Attention, Basis

4. Temperature, Creature, Worst, Climate, Sanctity

5. Newspaper, Important, Possible, World, Standard, Considered, Advantageous

6. Process. Morale, Contribution, Increased, Outsourcing

7. Though, Doctorates, Studies, Required, Country, Education

8. Students, Post-graduation, benefitted, Quality, Universities, Sophisticated, Students, Middle, Taught

9. Requires, Complete, Selected, Paragraph, Vocabulary, Sentence, Structure

10. Because, Rules, Window, Duolingo, Stringent, Taking, Additional

Task-4(20 Seconds for each statement)
Maximum no. of statements- 3

Record yourself saying a given statement – This task is not only about your pronunciation of individual words but also about your sentence stress and intonation knowledge. Remember that English is a stress-timed language which means that some syllables will be longer or shorter, so catch the real tone of the sentence.

Record yourself saying the statement below:

"We had not seen each other for twenty years."

Tip! Record yourself saying these sentences and listening back to them to see if you can improve your pronunciation.
Try these sentences recording and improving your pronunciation

- University departments should carefully monitor articles.
- The placement test for mathematics is offered in this semester.
- Animals raised in captivity behave differently.
- Mutually exclusive events are neither complementary nor opposing.
- Everyone must evacuate from the premises during the fire drill.
- The celebrated theory is still a subject of great controversy.
- Those students seeking a further extension should talk to their faculty.
- The basic underlying issue must be addressed.
- An aerial photograph was promptly registered.
- Control systems in manufacturing require a high level of accuracy.
- Native speakers are tested in the language test in their language.
- The university library has most of the necessary books.
- You are required to complete the research paper by next Monday.

<u>Task-5(30 Seconds for each statement)</u>
<u>Maximum no. of statements- 3</u>

Record yourself saying the statement You hear – This task is not only about your pronunciation of individual words but also about your sentence stress and intonation knowledge. Remember that English is a stress-timed language which means that some syllables will be longer or shorter, so in this task also catch the real tone

Tip! Record yourself saying these sentences and listening back to them to see if you can improve your pronunciation.
  - Your thesis should have fairly limited scopes.
  - The coffee house has a special student discount throughout the week.
  - All writers consciously or unconsciously all represent their culture.
  - The student's identification card will be issued today and tomorrow.
  - The qualification will be assessed with the criterion to approach.
  - It is important to allocate your time wisely when revising.
  - Leading companies changed their policies after reports are released.
  - Please remember to bring a highlighter to class next Monday.
  - Competition for the places in the course is fierce.
  - The theme of the work exhibits more of a demure compositional style.
  - If it helps to take notes to concentrate, please do so.
  - To gain full marks, an appropriate bibliography is required.
  - I thought we would meet in the small room.
  - The qualification will be assessed by using the reference approach.
  - The island is located in the south end of the bay.
  - Everyone must evacuate the premises during the fire drill.
  - The lecture on economic policy has been cancelled.
  - Sales figures for last year were better than expected.
  - The schedule allows plenty of time for independent study.
  - The application process is longer than expected.
  - The sociology department is highly regarded worldwide.
  - The economic books are at the back on the left.
  - Identity theft happens to thousands of people every year.

Task-6(15 seconds to prepare and
3 seconds to respond for each image)
Maximum no. of images- 6

Speak the English word for each image – This time instead of being given a word to pronounce you are being tested on your vocabulary knowledge as well as your general pronunciation. If you are unsure of the word for what you are seeing, you can always take a guess.

Tip! You are not penalized for making wrong answers, so always guess if you don't know!

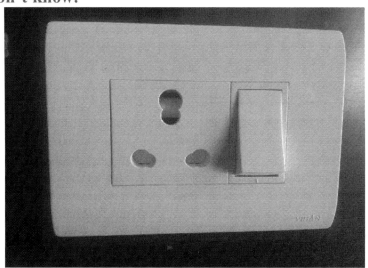

SWITCH BOARD/SWITCH

FIREPLACE

SCENERY

MONITOR

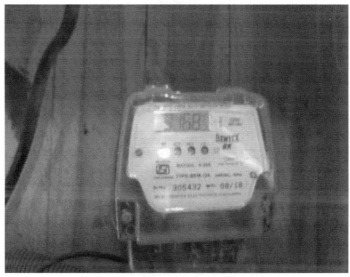

ELECTRIC METER

Students can expect some of these images

kitchen Utensils

Serving bowl · Mug · Jug · Spatula · Timer · Thermos

Bowl · Frying pan · Cup · Lid · Pan · Perforated spoon · Ladle · Blender

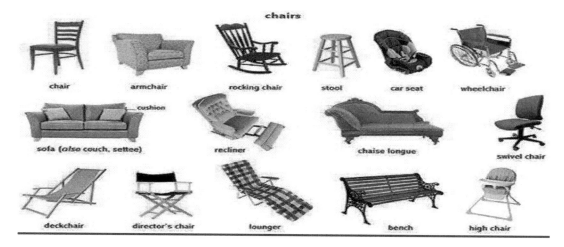

chairs

chair · armchair · rocking chair · stool · car seat · wheelchair

sofa (*also* couch, settee) · cushion · recliner · chaise longue · swivel chair

deckchair · director's chair · lounger · bench · high chair

Liquid soap	WC (water closet)	Wash tube	Wash basin	Toilet paper

Towels	Soaps	Soap holder	Toilet paper holder	Shower stall

Faucet	Shower	Dust pan & broom	Clothes	Cleaning tools

Stationery and Office Supplies

files | ring binder | folders | paper clips | Post-it™ | Bulldog clip™

fountain pen (nib) | staples | spiral bound | clip

pencil (lead) | staple remover | stapler | pencil sharpener | notebook | notepad | clipboard

ballpoint (*BrE* also Biro™) | card index (*BrE*) card catalog (*NAmE*) (index card) | correction fluid | eraser (*BrE* also rubber) | pushpins (*NAmE*) drawing pins (*BrE*) thumbtacks (*NAmE*)

highlighter (felt tip)

marker | glue stick | tape dipenser | Sellotape™ (*BrE*) Scotch tape™ (*NAmE*) | envelope (flap) | rubber band (*BrE* also elastic band) | rubber stamp (ink-pad) | hole punch

In the Living room

wing chair | TV stand | sofa | cushion

telephone | television | speaker | end table

sofa | cushion | TV stand | wing chair | telephone | television | speaker | end table | tea set | fireplace | remote | fan | table | carpet | floor lamp | picture | grandfather clock | curtains

chairs

chair   armchair   rocking chair   stool   car seat   wheelchair

cushion

sofa (*also* couch, settee)   recliner   chaise longue   swivel chair

deckchair   director's chair   lounger   bench   high chair

Liquid soap	WC (water closet)	Wash tube	Wash basin	Toilet paper
Towels	Soaps	Soap holder	Toilet paper holder	Shower stall
Faucet	Shower	Dust pan & broom	Clothes	Cleaning tools

Mammals

badger	bat	bear	bison	cow	deer
bull	calf	camel	cat	coyote	dog
donkey	elephant	fawn	fox	horse	hyena
giraffe	goat	gorilla	hippopotamus	kangaroo	zebra
leopard	lion	monkey	moose	rhinoceros	sheep
panda bear	pigs	polar bear	tiger	wolf	raccoon

Task-7(60 Seconds for each image)
Maximum no. of images- 3

Write one or more sentences about the given image - This task asks you to write complete sentences that have appropriate punctuation and give the reader an idea of what is being shown in the picture.

Tip! The more you can write in the short amount of time given, the higher mark you will receive.

Image1

Sample answer: A seminar is being held to promote some products or services, and surprisingly all the attendees are listening to the lecture attentively.

Image 2

Sample answer: A customer is inspecting the refrigerators at a showroom, and the manager is waiting for the response of the customer.

Image 3

Sample answer: Approximately ten students are attending their English class, and are busy in reading some contents.

Image 4

Sample answer: Many people are enjoying the party in a beautifully decorated hall, and are having their favorite meal.

Task-8(90 Seconds for each list)
Maximum no. of lists- 3

Choose the real words from an audio list – In this task, you listen to the words being given orally before selecting the real words.

Tip! The pronunciation might sound like a real word but in fact, it isn't, so listen to them very carefully!

Select the real English words in this list

🔊 WORD 1 ✓	🔊 WORD 2 ✓	🔊 WORD 3 ✓
🔊 WORD 4 ✓	🔊 WORD 5 ✓	🔊 WORD 6 ✓
🔊 WORD 7 ✓	🔊 WORD 8 ✓	🔊 WORD 9 ✓

You can expect some of these real words
Listen to these words in the talking dictionary and get used to listening to them

Ascend	Descend	Rail	Derail
Persuade	Dissuade	Assist	Resist
Clear	Bleary	Utility	Futility
Appreciate	depreciate	Sanity	Vanity
Ability	Disability	Solar	Lunar
Seed	Weed	Progress	Digress
Natal	Fatal	Project	Reject
Hale	Pale	Inject	Eject
Internal	external	Fame	Shame
Propose	Dispose	Jail	Bail
Arrange	Derange	Clinch	Flinch
Incline	Decline	Acrimony	Harmony
Increase	Decrease	Jot	Lot
Efficient	Deficient	Mercury	Murky
Micro	Macro	Approach	Reproach
Sapid	Vapid	Maternal	Paternal
Including	Excluding	Evolution	Revolution
Lazy	Crazy	Single	Mingle
Promote	Demote	Hire	Fire
Wild	Mild	Gravitation	Levitation
Employ	Deploy	Mortal	Immortal

Task-9 (5 minutes for each question)
Maximum no. of questions- 2

Respond to the question in at least 50 words. In this task, you will be given a statement on which you will have to write at least 50 words. You will have 5 minutes to respond, so write the best 50 words in terms of qualitative grammar and vocabulary

1 Example statement:
Communication has been changed significantly for the last 10 years.
Do you agree or not?

Sample answer:
Information technology has not only brought the world closer but also people can share information quickly and efficiently which was not possible in the past. The world has been developed into a global village due to the help of information technology allowing sharing ideas and information. Moreover, communication has also become cheaper, quicker, and more efficient. Hence, I completely acquiesce to the given statement.

2 Example statement:
Large shopping malls are replacing small shops. What is your opinion?

Sample answer:
In the modern era, people are motivated to buy their necessities from the competitive market. As a result, the number of shopping malls has been established for the past two decades in almost all cities of the world. There are reasons for people to believe that large shopping malls are important as a variety of options are available in one complex. For example, clothes, groceries, banks, pharmacies, cinemas, food courts, and restaurants, etc. are all available under a single roof and people get a better environment from such an establishment. As far as I am concerned, big shopping malls have immense benefits to the modern society that outweigh the options and conveniences offered by the small shops.

Task-10
Maximum no. of questions- 4

Prepare to speak for at least 30 seconds about the given question – This activity is similar to that of the IELTS Cue Card of the speaking module and gives you some prompts on the topic that they would like you to speak about. As the test is recorded using your webcam, the video is assessed and a mark is given for your fluency, accuracy, pronunciation, and how well you can get your point across.

Tip! If you cannot think of a true answer to the question then you can invent one. Don't get stuck thinking about, just choose the related contents that you know and go from there.

1. Describe a film that you would like to watch in the future.

What is the film called?

What is it about?

Where did you hear about this film from?

Why would You like to Watch it?

Sample answer:

I'm going to talk about a film that I'd like to watch when it comes out later this year. It's Salman khan's new film, and I saw in the news that it's going to be called 'Jahan'. I think 'Jahan' refers to the name of the imaginary region or the whole world.

As 'Jahan' hasn't been released yet, I don't know exactly what it will be about, but I can guess that the hero, Salman, is going to be on a mission to save his kingdom from an arch-criminal as usual. I'm sure it will be similar to most of the previous Salman's films, with a plotline involving lots of twists and turns, and with Salman using his skills to defeat his nemesis in the end.

Of course, Salman's films are unrealistic, you could even say ridiculous, but they're always fast, entertaining and fun, a bit like a roller-coaster ride!

Useful topics for discussion

Television

1. Do you think most people watch TV for education or entertainment?

I think people watch TV primarily for entertainment. There are far more entertainment programs than educational ones, and in my experience, most people treat television as a form of relaxation in the evening. If I think about the most popular TV programs in India, such as talent shows like 'India got talent' or soap operas like 'kahani ghar ghar ki', the focus is definitely on entertainment rather than education. Though some educational programs are very popular, in comparison, entertaining programs have a subtle influence on the minds of people.

2. Should TV play a role in educating children? How?

Yes, it definitely should play a role in my opinion. Good children's TV programs should tell stories that contain some kind of lesson about how to behave or what is morally right and wrong. Many of the traditional tales, such as 'vikram betal ', have been made into TV programs, and there is always a positive message in those stories.

3. How do you think TV viewing habits change as people get older?

TV viewing habits change a lot as we get older. While toddlers might watch programs about talking animals, teenagers prefer action and adventure or sports, and as adults, we start taking an interest in news and politics. My preferences, for example, have changed over the years - I would never have watched news programs when I was younger. I think it would be very strange if our viewing habits didn't mature!

Films

1. Do you think films have changed since you were a child?

No, I don't think films have changed much since I was a child. When I was younger I enjoyed watching action films, and the bollywood formula for this type of film seems to be the same today. For example, I liked the original 'Superman' films, and superheroes are still a popular subject for film-makers.

2. As the technology for home viewing improves, do you think people will stop going to the cinema in future?

No, I don't think that people will stop going to the cinema. People can already buy fantastic home viewing equipment, but it still feels more special to share the experience of watching a new film in a theatre full of people. I don't think that technology will be able to replicate that cinema atmosphere.

<u>Helping others</u>

1) What are some of the ways people can help others in the community? Which is the most important?

I think there are many ways to help others in our local communities. For example, where I live, some people volunteer to run activity clubs for children, or they help out in residential homes for elderly people. Others give money, food or clothes to organizations that support people living below the poverty line. In my opinion, there isn't a scale of importance when it comes to helping others; all forms of help are positive.

2) Why do you think some people like to help other people?

Most people get a good feeling when they help others, and they understand that we can all experience difficult times in our lives when we might need support. For example, we all grow old, and we all run the risk of losing our jobs or having a health problem that affects our ability to look after ourselves. So, I think people help others because they empathize with them.

3) Some people say that people help others in the community more now than they did in the past. Do you agree or disagree? Why?

I disagree with that kind of opinion. It's impossible to generalize about how much people help in their communities from one generation to the next, so I don't think we should try to judge or compare how altruistic people are now or were in the past. There have always been those who help others and those who don't.

Advice

1. Is it better to get advice from a friend or a family member?

I think it all depends on the kind of advice that you need. Parents and grandparents probably have more life experience than a friend, and so you might get a wiser or more sensible answer from them. On the other hand, friends are less likely to become too worried if you go to them with a problem. For example, I probably wouldn't want to burden my parents with a financial problem.

2. What would you say are the characteristics of a good adviser?

Well, firstly, a good adviser should be a good listener, someone who takes the time to understand the situation before offering advice. Secondly, an adviser should try to be objective, and avoid judging the person who is seeking help. Finally, I think the best advisers can ask the right questions and encourage others to find their answers.

3. Should people make their work and career decisions, or is it a good idea to ask for advice about this?

I'd say that it's a mixture of both things. Most of us talk to family, friends, teachers or colleagues before we make career choices. However, I believe that the final decision should rest with the individual; we all need to take ultimate responsibility for the big life choices that we make.

Holidays

1) Do you think that it's important for people to go on holiday?

Yes, I think we all need to go on holiday at least once or twice a year. It isn't healthy to work all year round without some time off to relax; we all need to take a break and recharge our batteries from time to time. Last summer, for example, I went on holiday to Shimla for a couple of weeks, and it was great to leave all of my usual responsibilities behind me. I came home feeling refreshed and reinvigorated.

2) Why do you think some people prefer not to go abroad on holiday?

I suppose there are different reasons why some people choose not to go abroad on holiday. Firstly, it's usually more expensive to travel abroad than it is to stay at home. A second reason could be that some people find it stressful to spend time in a foreign country where they don't speak the language.

Visitors

1. In your country, how do people treat visitors from abroad?

I think we treat visitors well. People in India are very open-minded and welcoming and believe in the concept of 'Atithi Devo Bhava', and people enjoy the mix of cultures that immigration and tourism bring. Most Indian metro cities, for example, are cosmopolitan, and you can meet visitors from every part of the world.

2. Do you think hospitality towards visitors is less important than it was in the past?

In my city, maybe it's true that hospitality is less important nowadays, but that's only because we are so used to seeing visitors from different countries, so we treat it as a normal part of life and nothing too special.

3. What are the advantages of staying with a friend compared to staying in a hotel when visiting a foreign country?

If you stay with a friend, you benefit from someone with local knowledge of the best places to visit. You can also get to know the character and customs of the local people, and for me, this is one of the most interesting aspects of a visit to another country. On the other hand, if you stay in a hotel, you are forced to discover the new place on your own, so it's more of an adventure.

Hobby

1. Do you think it's important for people to have hobbies? Why?

Yes, I think people need to have hobbies because we all need to do the things we enjoy in our spare time. In my case, I find that playing .... once a week with some friends and it helps me to relax, keep fit and forget about work and study. I think it's the same for everyone.

2. Can hobbies have any negative effects?

Yes, if you spend too much time on your hobby, it can affect other parts of your life. I remember that one of my friends spent most of his time at university playing computer games instead of studying. In the end, he failed most of his exams.

Events

1. What do you think we can learn by studying events of the past?

I think we can learn a lot by studying history. Just as individual people learn from their mistakes, societies can learn from the mistakes made by previous governments or leaders. For example, from what I've read in the newspapers, many economists are looking back to the time of the Great Depression, around 80 years ago, to understand the financial crisis that is currently affecting many countries around the world. Even if we don't always learn from mistakes, I think it's fascinating to study history because it gives us an insight into who we are and where we come from.

2. What important events do you think might take place in the future?

It's really difficult to predict what will happen in the future; most of the big, historic events of the past would have been impossible to foresee. For example, I don't think that anyone living 100 years ago could have imagined that people would one day walk on the moon! If I had to guess what might happen in the future, I'd like to think that scientists will invent cures for diseases like cancer, and we'll all live longer.

Rivers

1. What do you think are the functions of rivers nowadays?

Rivers have various functions. In India, they were probably more important in the past because they were used for irrigation and the transportation of goods and people, but I suppose this is still the case in many parts of the world. Rivers can be used as a source of renewable energy in the production of hydro-electric power, and they are also a source of freshwater for drinking. other functions are fishing, canoeing, swimming, bathing... I'm sure there are many other things I haven't thought of.

2. What do you think of boats and ships as forms of transportation?

I'm a huge fan of boats and ships. If I went abroad, I would like to get to my destination through the water apart from that ships are vital for the transportation of oil and other heavy cargo.

3. Why do some people like to live near rivers, lakes or the sea?

Well, the view is probably a major factor; most people like to look out to sea, or across a river or lake. I'd much prefer to look out of my window onto a natural landscape than an apartment building in a city. Then there's the lifestyle: if you live by the sea, for example, you can lie on the beach, go for a swim, or do water sports like surfing or waterskiing. I definitely wouldn't mind living near a beach at some point in my life!

<u>School Competition</u>

1. Why do you think some school teachers use competitions as class activities?

I think teachers use competitions to motivate children in their classes. I'm sure that teachers try all kinds of activities to engage their pupils, and competitions might be one of the best ways to keep children interested or get them excited. Children love winning things.

2. Is it a good thing to give prizes to children who do well at school? Why?

It might be a good idea to encourage children to do well in games or sports, but I don't think we should give children prizes for their academic work. Children need to learn that the reason for studying is to learn useful things that will help them in their lives. I don't like the idea of children thinking that they will only work hard if there is a prize.

3. Would you say that schools for young children have become more or less competitive since you were that age? Why?

I'd say that they have become more competitive since I was young. Children now have to take exams from a much younger age, so I think there is more of a focus on doing well in tests. Parents also seem to be getting more competitive; I think that many parents push their children to do extra homework rather than letting them play with friends.

<u>Emotions</u>

1. Do you think it's good to show your emotions when you're angry?

I think it depends on the situation and how you show your emotions. I find that if I'm angry with a friend or someone in my family, it's best to tell them what the problem is and try to express how I feel. However, I don't think it helps to argue with people when you're angry; it's better to control the anger and explain what's wrong.

2. In your opinion, do women show their emotions more than men?

The stereotypical view is that women are more emotional, and in my experience, there is some truth in this; my mother, for example, tends to show her feelings much more readily than my father. However, I'm sure that there are exceptions to the stereotype.

3. Why do you think men tend to show their emotions less than women?

Maybe it's because of the way we are brought up. I think that boys are often taught from an early age not to cry. Also, boys are aware that their friends might see it as a sign of weakness if they show their feelings. Perhaps girls are brought up to be more sensitive to their friends' feelings.

Life

1. Do you think people had easier lives 50 years ago?
Yes, maybe life was simpler and less stressful 50 years ago. The mobile phone didn't exist, so I suppose it was easier to forget about work at the end of the day because people couldn't contact you so easily.

2. Do you think life will be more stressful in the future?
Yes, it probably will be more stressful. As the world gets smaller, employees will probably have to travel to different countries more often and stay in touch with colleagues and clients all over the world. There will also be more competition for jobs and the cost of living will keep going up.

Economic effects on the lifestyle

1. What is the relationship between leisure and the economy?

Well, people spend a lot of money on all sorts of leisure activities nowadays, so I think leisure is a very important part of the economy of most countries. Leisure could be anything that people do in their free time, such as eating out, going to the cinema, watching a football match, or staying in a hotel. lacs of people are employed in these areas.

2. How does the economy benefit from people's leisure activities?

The leisure industry makes a huge contribution to the economy. It keeps millions of people in employment, and all of these employees pay their taxes and have money to spend on other goods and services. At the same time, most people spend some of their earnings on leisure activities, and this money, therefore, goes back into the economy.

3. Do men and women enjoy the same type of leisure activities?

Yes and no. I think both men and women enjoy things like eating in restaurants or going to the cinema, but I'm sure, other activities are more popular with one gender. For example, I think more men than women go to watch cricket matches.

Parties

1. What types of party do people have, and why are parties important?

People have parties to celebrate special occasions like birthdays, weddings, or the beginning of a new year. I think it's important to celebrate these things because they are landmarks in our lives. Parties are a good way to bring people together, and they have an opportunity to let off some steam.

2. Why do you think some people like parties but others hate them?

Most people like parties because they have a good time at them - eating a nice meal, chatting to friends, or having a dance. People who don't like them might find social situations difficult because they are shy, or maybe they don't enjoy having to make small talk with people they don't know.

3. Do you think parties will become more popular in the future?

No, I don't think anything will change. People have always had parties, and I'm sure they always will in the future. Humans need to socialize and enjoy themselves, and parties are one of the best ways to do that.

Wild animals

1. What effects do you think humans have on wild animals?

Humans have a huge impact on wild animals. We have destroyed a lot of natural habitats, and many animals are in danger of extinction. Tigers and rhinos, for example, are endangered species because of humans. The pollution and waste that we produce also affect animals. In some places, there are no fish in the rivers.

2. What measures could we take to protect wildlife?

I think we need stricter rules to protect natural areas and the wild animals that live there. For example, we should stop cutting down trees in the rain forest. National parks are a good idea because they attract tourists while protecting wildlife.

3. Is it the responsibility of schools to teach children about protecting wildlife?

Yes, schools can play a big part in educating children about this issue. Children should learn how to look after the natural environment. I think schools already teach children about endangered species and the destruction of rain forests, so hopefully, future generations will do a better job of protecting wildlife.

<u>Sports</u>

1. Why do you think sport is important?

I think sport is important for different reasons. For me, doing a sport is about having fun. When I play…………….…..., I forget about everything else and just enjoy myself. Also, doing a sport helps you to keep fit and healthy, and it's a good way to socialize and make friends.

2. Do you think famous sportspeople are good role models for children?

I think that sportspeople should be good role models. Children look up to their favorite cricket players, like Sachin Tendulkar, so I think that these people have an enormous responsibility. They should try to be good and they should present an exemplary character to the world, and behave in the right way.

3. Do you agree that sports stars earn too much money?

In my opinion, it's fair that the best sportspeople earn a lot of money. Being a top sportsperson requires hours of practice, and there are millions of sports fans who are willing to pay to see them playing. If we don't want sportspeople to earn so much money, we shouldn't go to watch them.

<u>Good lesson</u>

1. What do you think makes a good lesson?

I think a good lesson is one that is interesting and engaging. By 'engaging' I mean that the students should feel involved in the lesson; they should feel that they are learning something new that is relevant to them. In my opinion, a lot depends on how the teacher delivers the content of the lesson in a way that students like. My favorite teacher at college/school/university used to involve the students by making us teach some of the lessons ourselves.

2. Do you think it's better to have a teacher or to teach yourself?

Well, there's no substitute for a good teacher. Though you can teach yourself, you can learn a lot more quickly under the guidance of a teacher. For example, when learning a language, you need someone to correct your mistakes; you can get the grammar and vocabulary from books, but books can't tell you where you're going wrong.

3. Do you think the traditional classroom will disappear in the future?

I don't think it will disappear, but it might become less common. I think more people will study independently, using different technologies rather than sitting in a classroom. Maybe students will attend a lesson just once a week, and spend the rest of their time following online courses or watching video lessons.

<u>Organisation</u>

What kinds of organizations regularly conduct questionnaires?

All kinds of organizations and companies use questionnaires to find out what people think about them. For example, university lecturers often ask their students to answer questions about their courses. Someone from a Coffee and café restaurant stopped me in the street yesterday to ask me about my coffee drinking habits.

Do you think schools should ask children for their opinions about lessons?

On the one hand, it might be useful for teachers to get feedback from children about how much they learnt and how enjoyable they found the lessons. However, children don't necessarily know what's best for them, and it might do more harm than good to allow them to give opinions about their teachers.

<u>Task-11</u>
<u>Maximum no. of questions- 2</u>

Prepare to speak for at least 1-3 minutes about the given image –
This activity is similar to that of PTE's Describe an image of the speaking module. As the test is recorded using your webcam, the video is assessed and a mark is given for your fluency, accuracy, pronunciation and how well you can get your point across.

Tip! Keep speaking what you see in the image. Don't get stuck.

Sample answer

As a child, I enjoyed playing chess. I think chess is probably the best-known board game in the world. It's a game for two players, and the aim is to defeat the other player by taking his or her pieces and eventually trapping his King. This final move is called checkmate.

I remember that it was a classmate of mine at primary school who first taught me to play chess. He had a small, portable chess set, and once I knew how each piece moved, we started playing at break and lunchtimes; we played in our classroom or outside on the school playground. Later, my parents bought me my own chess set as a birthday present so that I could play at home.

I liked playing chess because I enjoyed the challenge of thinking ahead and trying to outwit my opponent. I was probably seven or eight years old when I started playing, and it seemed like a very mysterious and intellectual game at that time. Also, although I loved winning, chess taught me to learn from my losses and to congratulate the person who had beaten me.

Sample answer

I'm going to talk about my primary school. The school was called .....
,and it was in the town of ..... . The location of the school was great
because it was within walking distance of our family home at the time.
The route to school was all downhill, which made it an easy walk in the
morning, but a tiring journey on the way home in the afternoon!

I was a student at ..... school between the ages of 5 and 11 - the full 6
years of primary education. From age 11 onwards, I went to a nearby
secondary school.

My primary school seemed like a big place at the time, but it was quite a
small school, with only six classes. I remember there being a large room
called the assembly hall, where the whole school gathered every morning
to hear messages from the headmaster. I also remember spending a lot of
time on the playground and the sports field. I liked all of my teachers;
they were caring but strict at the same time, and I think they fostered a
positive and fun atmosphere in the school.

I have elated memories of my primary school years, mainly because of
the friends I made, and the fun I had.

Task-12
Maximum no. of questions- 4

Prepare to speak for 1-3 about the questions you hear – This activity is similar to that of IELTS Cue Card of speaking module and task 10, and makes you answer 3-4questions you. The test is recorded using your webcam, the video is assessed and a mark given for your fluency, accuracy and pronunciation.

Tip! If you cannot think of a true answer to the question then you can invent one. Don't get stuck thinking about the real one, just choose one that you know and go from there.

Describe a prize that you would like to win. You should explain

What is the prize for?
How did you come to know about it?
What would you have to do to win it?
Why would you like to win this prize?

Sample answer:

I'm going to talk about a prize that I would like to win, which is the 'Student of the year' award at the institute where I study. At the end of December each year, the institute's director presents this award to a student who has scored the highest Duolingo English test score over the previous twelve months.

I first heard about this prize during my training and orientation period just after I got the admission three months ago. It was early December and some of my friends in the institute were discussing who might be awarded 'student of the year' later that month. I was intrigued and asked them to tell me more about the award.

As I said, the prize is given for 'outstanding performance in the Duolingo English test. I don't have an exact idea of what other qualities they look for, but I assume that you have to achieve certain standards, such as 100% attendance, good punctuality, and so on.

I'd like to win 'student of the year' because it would mean that my efforts had been recognized by the company directors, and this would help me to progress in my career. It would also give me a great sense of personal achievement.

Describe an aim or goal that you hope to achieve in the future.
You should say

What is the aim?
When do you hope to achieve it?
What do you need to do to reach your goal?

Sample answer:

I'm going to describe the future aim of mine, which is to write a novel. I'd like to write a novel, so the story or plot would be fictional, but it would probably be influenced by some of my own experiences, ideas and views.

Unfortunately, I have no idea where to start or what my novel would be about, so I can't imagine achieving this aim until later in my life. Maybe it will be something that I do as a hobby when I retire, or I might suddenly be inspired to start writing much sooner. It's just a vague objective at the moment.

I think it must be extremely difficult to find the motivation to write a novel, so more than anything I would need time, commitment and the passion to keep working until I finished. I would probably need to set a goal of writing for a certain amount of time each day, and of course, I'd need a good idea for a story in the first place.

Interview section (This section is not graded, but it is very important)

Task-1

Choose one topic out of two to speak about for 1-3 minutes – In this task, push yourself and demonstrate your English, try to include interesting language, complex grammar structures and discourse markers. This part isn't marked and part of your exam result, but it is sent to the institutions that you apply for. This is a great opportunity to show them who you are and your English skills.

Tip! Don't forget about your pronunciation and sentence intonation while

speaking.

Topic one

Describe an interesting conversation you had with someone you didn't know. You should say

Sample Answer:

I'm going to talk about an interesting conversation that I had a couple of weeks ago in a music shop. I was walking along with one of the main shopping streets in the city center, when a large window displaying all sorts of musical instruments caught my eye. Out of curiosity, I decided to go in and have a look around.

The person I ended up speaking to was a shop assistant on the second floor, in the area of the shop dedicated to acoustic guitars. I hadn't intended to speak to anyone, but the assistant approached me in a friendly way and asked whether I had any questions.

I explained to the assistant that I hadn't played the guitar for years, but that I wondered what the differences were between the various acoustic guitars on show. He talked to me about the different makes and models, whether they were factory or hand- made, the woods and varnishes used, the variation in sound quality, and of course the price range.

I found the conversation fascinating because the shop assistant was so knowledgeable. It was obvious that he had a passion for the guitar, and he didn't mind talking to me even though I had made it clear that I didn't intend to buy anything. He even picked up and played three or four of the instruments to demonstrate the differences in their sound.

Topic two

Describe an open-air or street market that you enjoyed visiting. You should say:

Sample Answer

I'm going to describe a street market that I've enjoyed visiting many times in Kurukshetra. It's the Sector-17 Market. The market showrooms are spread across several sites in the city center, but the centerpiece is the large shopping mall named Kessal Mall.

The Sector-17 Market stalls sell an array of gifts and mouth-watering food. It's a great place to find handmade crafts such as jewelry, ornaments, wooden toys and other souvenirs, but it's the food that seems to be most popular.

The market was originally quite small, occupying just one of the central squares in Kurukshetra, but it's grown quickly in recent years, spilling over into maybe five other pedestrian streets and a few other squares. There are over 20 stalls 100 showrooms now, so it's become a really big event attracting thousands of visitors.

The main reason I've always enjoyed visiting the Sector-17 Market is the fantastic ambiance and hustle and bustle. When I go there, it doesn't matter how cold or wet the weather is, Sector-17 Market seems to come alive when the market opens; the streets are bustling with people and there is a real festive feel in the city.

Task-2

Choose one topic out of two to write about for 3-5 minutes – This is the task where you will be able to show off your excellent writing skills about either of the given topics. You are also given prompts about what to include so you're being tested on your instruction following skills as well. Try to write for as long as possible (5 minutes and 500 words is the maximum limit) to make sure that you demonstrate your writing style and general English knowledge.

Tip! You should aim to use linking words, descriptive and imaginative language and complete sentences with complex grammar structures. For this task, you need to understand the functional and the basic grammar rules, so read the rules religiously.

Topic-one

Sample Answer:

Learning a new language at an early age is helpful for children. Is it more positive for their future aspect or have some adverse effects?

Research shows that learning a new language at an early age, maybe as early as 3 years old, opens up a whole new world for the child that otherwise would be difficult. I am of the view that it is more positive for their future.

The scientists believe that children have enhanced creativity, better memory and multi-tasking abilities at a younger age. At such an early age, it is much easier for the children to learn a new language with better fluency, accent than if they learn later in life. Children "soak everything like a sponge", this mantra in itself is proof that children are better learners than adults.

Children's brains are in the development age so they are ready to accept and willing to learn a foreign language. It can also provide academic benefits at a later stage in life. The studies show that bilingual students have higher mathematical skills and are known to perform better in exams including the SAT.

Unlike other parts of the body, our brain functions better with exercise. Learning a new language is more like an exercise for children as it involves memorizing rules and vocabulary. Overall it helps strengthen the brain. Bilingual (or multilingual) individuals have an edge in their school time, in college days and predominantly, in the workforce.

To conclude, the individuals who know two or more languages have better insight into people, places, and culture than the rest of those who don't. In turn, it enriches one's life and enhanced personal experiences in the world. Hence, I must say that learning a foreign language at an early age is useful for children.

Topic-Two

Sample answer:

It is usually foolish to get married before completing your studies and getting established in a good job? Do you agree or disagree"?

All over the world, it can be noticed that most adults get married before finishing their higher education over the past few decades. It is argued that getting married while studying or before getting a stable job can be arduous at times. This will be shown by analyzing how it can affect a person's studies and employment.

Marriage is a huge responsibility and one should be prepared for all the challenges associated with it. The responsibility of a spouse can augment a person's chores to a greater degree. For an instance, a married person has to take out some time for his studies to spend with his spouse, whereas a single person can focus on his studies and has the advantage to score higher grades. When looking at this example it is clear that marriage is a hindrance for a student. From this, it can be concluded that it's better to delay marriage and focus on academics.

Additionally, the initial stages of work-life are usually grueling. One has to spend a considerable amount of hours to get established in a good job. A relevant example I would like to mention is that a person settling up in a job may have to travel to different locations or branches. If the spouse is dependent, it can be tough to be flexible to cater to the demands of the workplace. When looking at this example it is obvious that it is foolish to get married before getting a stable job.

To recapitulate, I believe that education and financial security make an individual truly eligible for marriage. These factors are a necessity to live a healthy and desirable life.

STUDENTS CAN EXPECT THESE TYPES OF WRITING TOPICS

1. Some people prefer to spend time with one or two close friends. Others choose to spend time with a large number of friends. Compare the advantages of each choice. Which of these two ways of spending time do you prefer? Use specific reasons to support your answer.

Friends are people who support us through our lives. Some people prefer to have one or two close friends. However, others prefer to spend their time with many friends. I think that the number of friends depends on one's personality. I prefer to have a couple of close friends. In this essay, I will analyze both cases and present my view in favor of having a few close friends.

First of all, a person can establish closer relationships with a few friends. They can spend their time together, relax, and watch a movie in a silence that does not feel awkward. Second of all, close friends have a more familiar atmosphere. They can share many beautiful moments and thoughts. For example, I have only two close friends - my husband and my class-mate. I can share my worries and great news and can tell everything to them.

On the other side, having many friends can be hard and stressful. One has to spend his or her time with each of them. I think it is not healthy because a person does not have time to relax and contemplate his/her own life. I know these types of people. They like to be in the center of everyone's attention. They talk a lot, make jokes, and tell stories and rumors. They just play and pretend to be friends with other people. There is no doubt they succeed in it, but they spend so much time listening to other's worries and troubles and entertaining them that they practically do not have time for themselves.

To sum up, I agree with the statement that "a friend in need is a friend indeed". I am sure that my close friends will always help me and never betray or turn me down. However, a large number of friends do not allow establishing close and deep relationships.

2. Some people think that children should begin their formal education at a very early age and should spend most of their time in school studies. Others believe that young children should spend most of their time playing. Compare these two views. Which view do you agree with? Why?

People learn through their entire lives. Curiosity has always been the basic characteristic of a human being. We always want to break limits and learn more. At this point, some people think that children should begin their formal education at a very early age and spend most of their time on school studies. This will help them to succeed in the future. However, for several reasons, which I will explain below, I think that children should not study at a very early age.

Children who begin to study at a very early age have more chances to succeed in the future. They gain more knowledge and experience which are priceless and valuable. Besides, studying more now will allow them to perfect their knowledge in the future and become better professionals.

However, I think that every child must have his or her childhood. Children should learn through playing and communicating with their friends and parents. I think that such basic qualities as kindness, self-confidence and just a good sense of humor cannot be gained from studying. Children should more time spend with their family, playing and learning with their parents. Imagine that a child instead of playing with his friends does his homework and feel exhausted and tired. Another important aspect of this is that children at an early age need more exercise because at this age the development of their body is a very essential aspect. Children first of all must be healthy.

To sum up, I think that children should have a careless childhood with no responsibilities. Moreover, I am sure that playing helps them develop not only their bones and muscles but their ability to make decisions, analyze things, make conclusions, which is very good for their future.

3. Some people believe that university students should be required to attend classes. Others believe that going to classes should be optional for students. Which point of view do you agree with? Use specific reasons and details to explain your answer.

There are two points of view on this question. Some people believe that students are adults and they have their responsibilities, so they should have freedom in arranging their time. Other people think that optional attendance has a corruption effect on the educational system as a whole. I think that this question is more complicated.

First of all, many students have already children, so they sometimes have to skip a class or two to perform their responsibilities. Second of all, many students do not have enough money for their needs and they have to work more than other students. In this case, optional attendance is well-taken. Another important aspect of this subject that sometimes lectures of a particular teacher may be dry and uninteresting. I believe that it is reasonable to skip those classes and learn all by themselves. It can save time, so a person can spend it on research or preparation for a coming test.

On the other side, I think that some students who do not have any responsibilities may skip classes without any reason. They can have more time to attend clubs and parties. It harms their grades. So, it can result in a waste of money and time. Students may take the same classes more than one time to meet the requirements of their program. It is a waste of money for both a government and a family. A government will lose money because they are spent on education and it means they are tax-free. At the same time, parents will have to pay for the education of their child one more time. Another important aspect of this that students will not learn how to arrange their time to have all things done on time.

To conclude, I think that students must attend classes. However, some students with children or who have excellent grades and already work in the field of their major should be allowed to skip a particular amount of classes.

4. Should a city try to preserve its old, historic buildings or destroy them and replace them with modern buildings? Use specific reasons and examples to support your opinion.

Some people think that old, historic buildings are no need for the city and they should be destroyed and replaced with modern ones. However, other people believe that historic buildings must be preserved to know and remember our past. For several reasons, I agree with those people who want to preserve old, historical buildings.

First of all, by preserving historical buildings we pass our history to our future generations. I think that our children should know their history, learn from it and respect it. People need to know their traditions and customs, which are priceless and irreplaceable. Our history is our knowledge and power. In my opinion, we need to preserve and restore historical buildings. By destroying them we show our disrespect to our forefathers and their traditions.

Second of all, preserving historical buildings in a city can attract many travelers. Welcoming tourists a city can get many benefits including money, which can be spent on preserving historical buildings as well as on improving roads and facilities.

Also, many tourists mean a lot of new business opportunities. Another important aspect of this is that businessmen will be willing to build new recreational centers, hotels, movie theaters, shopping centers to make a city more attractive for travelers. In addition to those practical benefits, many people will have the opportunity to get a job. All this is good for the economy of the city.

To sum up, I believe that preserving old, historical buildings can bring only benefits to a city and all humankind.

4. Some people prefer to plan activities for their free time very carefully. Others choose not to make any plans at all for their free time. Compare the benefits of planning free-time activities with the benefits of not making plans. Which do you prefer - planning or not planning for your leisure time? Use specific reasons and examples to explain your choice.

Nowadays, people have so many things to do that they almost always do not have enough time for it. When we go to bed we carefully think and plan our next day and it continues day in and day out. We wake up, recollect our checklist with things to do and in a few minutes, we are already in a car on our way to the office. People often do not have time for themselves, so when people have some spare time they want to use it wisely. Some people prefer to plan activities for their free time very carefully. However, others prefer not to make any plans. In this essay, I will analyze both cases and present my view in favor of planning free-time activities.

On the one side, not making any plans and just letting the time pass by for some time have some benefits. First of all, a person can just relax, enjoy the beautiful moments, spend his or her time with loved ones, watch a movie, listen to relaxing music, observe the flowers in bloom from the window, contemplate about his or her life and just slow down the pace of life. I think it is a very good way to eliminate one's stress and tension and just leave all troubles and worries behind.

On the other side, careful planning can bring many benefits too. First of all, one can travel. However, traveling requires some planning to be made. For example, one most likely will need a hotel room. So, the reservation should be made beforehand. Also, it is wise to check one's car to avoid breakdowns and have an uninterrupted worry-free trip. Second of all, planning one's activities allows spending one's free time the way he/she likes. For instance, if I want to play tennis on the incoming weekend, I will certainly make a reservation for a court because in this case I will not be disappointed with the waste of my time. I prefer to make plans for my free time because it allows me to spend my vacation or week-ends the way I want it.

To sum up, I think careful planning allows people to derive maximum benefits from their free time. However, I must confess sometimes I allow myself just to stay at home with my friends and family and not make any plans.

6. Some people prefer to work for themselves or own a business. Others prefer to work for an employer. Would you rather be self-employed, work for someone else, or own a business? Use specific reasons to explain your choice.

People work for money and self-realization. However, some people prefer to be self-employed and others prefer to work for an employer. These two options are very different. I think that each of them has its advantages and disadvantages.

Working as an employee brings many benefits. First of all, one can spend more time with his family helping his child do his homework, fishing with the whole family, etc. Second of all, one has fewer responsibilities. He just does his job and does not care about the market, competitors and expected profit. One taking a vocation can forget about all troubles, relax and not worry about who does his job during his absence. Finally, an employee can always find a more interesting job with a higher salary.

On the other side, be self-employed have many benefits too. First of all, one knows the more he works the more he gets. Another important reason for being self-employed is independence. One does not have to report to anyone except one's self. However, in addition to these practical benefits, one gets more responsibilities to take care of.

To sum up, I think that be self-employed is not as easy as it may seem. A person must be self-confident, strong, and patient. He must know exactly what he wants and be ready to sacrifice all his spare time to it. I have a family and at this moment, I am not sure that I am ready to sacrifice my time to the job.

IMPORTANCE OF KNOWING SPELLINGS, AND UNCOMMON WORDS

Learning different words becomes essential when someone wants to have mastery over the language, other than one's mother tongue. Specifically, the students who are appearing for **DUOLINGO** must know the common and uncommon words of the English language as the grading in Task 3 depends on the appropriate usage of lexical resources.

As all the words of the English language may be difficult to learn, it is imperative to learn at least 800-1000 words which are important to communicate in the English language.

Keeping in view the levels of common students, in this red color section, some of the common and uncommon words are compiled to enhance the spelling power and lexical resource of the students. These words will be of great help to complete the different tasks of Duolingo very easily with a higher level of confidence.

IMPORTANT WORDS AND THEIR SPELLINGS FOR DUOLINGO

Days of the week:

Monday, Tuesday, Wednesday, Thursday, Friday, Saturday, Sunday,

Months of the year:

January, February, March, April, May, June, July August, September, October, November, December

Money matters:

cash, debit, credit card, bankers cheque, in advance, annual fee, monthly membership, interest rate, deposit, tuition fees, poverty, bank statement, money management, current account, student account, withdraw, low-risk investment, mortgage, grace period, budget deficit, retail voucher, coupon, counterfeit money, public money, taxpayers' money, debt, interest-free credit, purchase, partial refund, annuity, non-refundable, MasterCard, VISA, distribution costs, income, finance department, family finances, duty-free store

Subjects:

science, politics, history, biology, architecture, law, geography, archaeology, literature, business management, agriculture, statistics, mathematics, logic, physics, psychology, anthropology, economics, philosophy, performing arts, visual arts, chemistry, humanities

Studying at college/university:

Course outline, group discussion, handout, written work, report writing, research, Proofreading, experiment, experience, reference, textbook, dictionary, laptop, printer, student advisor, teamwork, module, topic, assessment, library, department, computer center, classroom, lecture, tutor, main hall, attendance, deadline, Speech, computer laboratory, certificate, diploma, placement test, overseas students, full-time, facilities, college, dining room, specialist, knowledge, international, accommodation, primary, secondary, intermediate, media room, resources room, staff, commencement, dissertation, leaflet, faculty, pupils, pencil, feedback, tasks, outcomes, advanced, introductory, extra background, higher education, guidelines, post-secondary, supervisor, bachelor's degree, compound, vocabulary, student support services, student retention, publication, foreign students, schedule, school reunion, registrar's office

Marketing:

catalog, interview, newsletter, competition, TV program, strategies, research method, entertainment industry, leadership, management, display, products, customer, special offer, collecting data, questionnaire, survey, mass media, statistics, profit margin, poll, business card, training, trainee, merchandise, manufacture, recruitment

Health:

yoga, tai-chi, keep-fit, salad bar, vegetarian, outdoor activities, leisure time, disease, meal, protein, balanced diet, food pyramid, vitamin, carbohydrates, rice, pasta, potatoes, pizza, tomatoes, bread, cereals, minerals, zinc, meat, seafood, eggs, beans, milk, cheese, yogurt, fruit, vegetables, citrus fruits, green pepper, black current, nuts, egg yolk, liver, medicine, treatment, remedy, nursing care, nursery, regular exercise

Nature:

field, footbridge, environment, waterfall, river, mountain, forest, village, coast, reef, lake, valley, hill, cliff, island, peninsula, earthquake, avalanche, tornado, typhoon, desertification, volcano, disaster, catastrophe, erosion, landslides, storm, flood, hurricane, pond, jungle, oasis, dam, canyon

The environment:

greenhouse effect, acid rain, global warming, carbon dioxide, burning fossil, exhaust fumes, deforestation, nitrogen oxide, smog, climate, pollution, temperature, power plants, landfill, cattle, wind turbine, solar power, hydroelectric power, renewable, source of energy, reliable, solar panels

The animal kingdom:

birds of prey, seabirds, poultry and game, mammals, cetacean, whale, primates, rodents, fish, amphibian, reptile, insects, octopus, phylum, class, order, family, genus, species, livestock, creature, lion, penguin,

Plants:

Mushroom, fungus, leaves, seed, core, bark, trunk, twig, branch, flower, stem, roots, cluster, fertilizer

Continents:

South America, North America, Africa, Asia, Europe, Australia and Antarctica

Languages:

Linguistics, bilingual, trilingual, polyglot, Portuguese, Mandarin, Bengali, Chinese, Hindi, Russian, Japanese, German, Punjabi, Thai, Persian, Filipino, French, Italian, Greek,

Architecture and buildings:

Dome, palace, fort, castle, glasshouse, pyramid, long cabin, lighthouse, hut, skyscraper, sculpture

Homes:

semi-detached house, duplex, terraced house, townhouse, row house, bungalow, thatched cottage, mobile home, houseboat, block of flats, apartment building, condominium, chimney, bedroom, basement, landlord, tenant, rent, lease, neighborhood, suburb, sofa, coffee table, dormitory, storey, kitchen, refrigerator, microwave, ground floor, oven, hallway, insurance

In the city:

Cities, street, lane, city center, central station, car park, department store, bridge, temple, embassy, road system, hospital, garden, avenue

Workplaces:

Clinic, dentist, reception, appointment, staff selection, colleague, workshop, showroom, information desk, employer, employment, unemployed, technical cooperation, team leaders, stress, ability, vision, confidence, employee, internship

Rating and qualities:

Reasonable, satisfactory, dangerous, safe, strongly recommended, poor quality, satisfied, disappointed, efficient, luxurious, colored, spotted, striped, expensive, cheap

Touring:

Tourist guided tour, ticket office, souvenir, trip, guest, reservation, view, culture, memorable, single double-bedded room, picnic, tourist attraction, hostel, suite, aquarium

Verbs:

Train, develop, collect, supervise, mark, edit, revise, exhibit, donate, surpass, register, support, hunt, persuade, concentrate, discuss, suggest, arrange, borrow, immigrate, review, learn, touch.

Adjectives:
energetic, social, ancient, necessary, fantastic, exciting, fabulous, dull, comfortable, convenient, suitable, affordable, voluntary, temporary, permanent, Immense, vast, salty, extinct, vulnerable, pessimistic, optimistic, realistic

Hobbies:
orienteering, caving, spelunking, archery, ice skating, scuba diving, snorkeling, skateboarding, bowls, darts, golf, billiards, photography, painting, pottery,

Sports:
Cricket, baseball, basketball, rugby, soccer, American football, hockey, swimming, tennis, squash, badminton, ping-pong, field, court, pitch, stadium, team, the discus, the javelin, the hammer, the high jump, horse racing, show jumping, polo, cycling, gymnasium, athlete, gym, extreme sports, paragliding, hang-gliding, skydiving, boarding, white-water rafting, kite surfing, mountain biking, jogging, press-up, push-up, barbell, treadmill, judo, recreation, snooker, walking, championship, **Shapes:**
Square, rectangular, triangular, polygon, oval, spherical, spiral, circular, curved, cylindrical

Measurement
Width, length, altitude, imperial system, metric system, Mass, depth, breadth, height, three dimensions, frequency

Transportations:
Argo plane, shipment, container ship, boat, lifeboat, ferry, hovercraft, hydrofoil, liner, canal boat, narrowboat, dinghy sailing, sailboat, paddle steamer, cabin cruiser, rowing boat, rowboat, kayak, canoe, punt, gondola, aircraft, helicopter, seaplane, airship, hot-air balloon, airport, crew, passenger, platform, hire a car, automobile

Vehicles:
Double-decker bus, single-decker, minibus, school bus, coach, truck, tanker, van, lorry, transporter, forklift truck, tow truck, breakdown truck, pickup, jeep, caravan, camper, tractor, taxi, cab, tram, underground, subway, stream train, freight train, goods train,

Weather: Humid, hot, sticky, breeze, chilly, cold, cool, dry, dusty, freezing, hot, warm, wet, weather forecast, antenna, moisture.

Places:
the local library, swimming pool, cafeteria, cottage, parliament, accommodation, restaurant, canteen, cafe, bookshop, sports center, city council, dance studio, park, conversation club, kindergarten

Equipment and tools:
Helmet, light, musical instrument, cassette, silicon chip, digital monitor, gadget, device, screen, breaks, wheels, mechanical pencil, disk, backpack

The arts and media:
Opera, orchestra, concert, symphony, the press, conductor, vocalist, audience, festival, carnival, exhibition, classical music, theatre, cinemas, art gallery, museum

Materials:
fur, metal, steel, aluminum, copper, rubber, plastic, ceramics, glass, cement, stone, textile, cotton, fabric, wool, leather, bone, paper, lumber/wood, glue, composite, fiberglass, concrete, wax, paper, wood, silver, gold, feather

Works and jobs:
occupation, profession, designer, decorator, architect, engineer, manager, waitress, waiter, teacher, vacancy, professor, specialist, psychologist volunteer, freelance, secretary, craftsman, work experience, curriculum vitae, mail address, receptionist, pilot, guard, flight attendant

Colors:
Blue, white, orange, green, grey, black, red, yellow, purple, brown, pink

Expressions and time:
three times, three times per week, a gap year, full-time, part-time, midday, midnight, millennium, century, decade, fortnight.

Miscellaneous:
passport photo, state, government, individual, variety, private sector, practice, gender, creativity, original inhabitant, indigenous, demonstration, strike, entrance, circuit, guarantee, dialogue, commerce, carriage, narrative, chocolate, satellite, decision, prototype, attitude, daily routine, personal fulfillment, activity, recipient, ultrasound, pedestrian safety, traffic jams, procedures, creation, prize, junior-senior, opportunity, driving license, process, literary, man-made, republicans, umbrella, frequently updated, waiting list, sewer systems, liberal democracy, democrats, lunar calendar, libertarian, burger, videos, nature conservation, life.

IMORTANT VOCABULARY FOR DUOLINGO

WORDS	MEANING
Diligent	Hardworking
Wilt	Collapse
Indolent	Lazy
Abandon	To give up
Cite	Quote
Besiege	Surround
Conducive	Suitable
Marvelous	Wonderful
Morbid	Diseased
Repercussion	Reaction
Entice	Tempt
Severe	Rigid
Modish	Stylish
Restoration	Reestablish
Impeccable	Faultless
Paramount	Supreme
Licentious	Immoral
Simon-pure	Genuine
Ambience	Environment
Exhausted	Tired
Denounce	Talking against
Specious	Insincere
Profound	Deep
Foster	Nurture
Filthy	Dirty
Nostalgic	Homesick
Oversee	Supervise
Deceive	Mislead, cheat
Prerogative	Privilege

Radiant	Bright
Hoodlum	Criminal
Spasmodic	Intermittent
Maunder	Wander
Dowdy	Weird
Reckless	Rash
Contemplative	Thoughtful
Nepotism	Favoritism
Liberal	Generous
Interim	Temporary
Hoodwink	Deceive
Rampant	Prevalent
Aberration	A change
Inept	Novice
Arrogant	Adamant
Acquiesce	Agree
Decry	Disagree
Endorse	Support
Zenith	Top most
Nadir	Lowest
Exhibit	To display
Maze	Proverb
Optimist	Positive
Pessimist	Despondent
Inflation	A rise in price
Sedentary	Comfortable
Paragon	perfect example
Candor	Straight forward
Erudite	Scholar
Amazing	Surprising

Evidence	Proof
Ruckus	Loud noise
Stupendous	Splendid
Assiduous	Hard work
Abhor	Hate
Astonish	Surprising
Abate	Reduced
Gregarious	Friendly
Comprehend	Understand
Concrete	Solid
Dissuade	To discourage
Assent/consent	Agree
Dissent	Disagree
Despondent	Pessimist
Panacea	universal remedy
amicable	Friendly
appease	Satisfy , gratify
avarice	Greedy
chide	Mild scolding
deride	To make fun
elated	joyful
enmity	Deep ill – will
extol	To praise, glorify, or honor

FUNCTIONAL GRAMMAR: LESSON -1

TO BE (USE OF IS/AM/ARE, WAS/WERE, WILL BE/SHALL BE)

TO DESCRIBE SOMETHING

When we want to describe something, or we want to make sentences which do not involve any sense of action, the sentences can be formed by using is/am/are in the present tense, by using was/were in the past sense, and by using will be/shall be in the future sense.

हम कुछ का वर्णन करना चाहते हैं, या हम वाक्यों को बनाना चाहते हैं जिसमें क्रियाओं की कोई भावना शामिल नहीं है

Present sense
- Ajay is my friend.

- I am an English teacher.

- They are my students.

- He is an intelligent student.

- They are football players.

Past sense
- Earlier, I was an engineer.

- We were IELTS students.

- He was ill yesterday.

- They were late today.

Future sense
- In the future, I shall be a director.

- We will be very happy.

- I shall be late tomorrow.

The use of different helping verbs:

SUBJECTS	IS/AM/ARE	WAS/WERE	WILL BE/SHALL BE
I	AM	WAS	SHALL BE
WE	ARE	WERE	SHALL BE
YOU	ARE	WERE	WILL BE
HE	IS	WAS	WILL BE
SHE	IS	WAS	WILL BE
IT	IS	WAS	WILL BE
THEY	ARE	WERE	WILL BE
SINGULAR NOUN	IS	WAS	WILL BE
PLURAL NOUN	ARE	WERE	WILL BE

We can make negative and interrogative sentences by just adding not with the helping verbs or shifting the helping verbs before the subjects.

	PRESENT IS/AM/ARE	PAST WAS/WERE	FUTURE WILL BE/ SHALL BE
(+) (-) (?)	HE IS A DOCTOR. HE IS NOT A DOCTOR. IS HE A DOCTOR?	HE WAS ILL YESTERDAY. HE WAS NOT ILL YESTERDAY. WAS HE ILL YESTERDAY?	I SHALL BE BUSY. I SHALL NOT BE BUSY. SHALL I BE BUSY?
(+) (-) (?)	I AM A NURSE. I AM NOT A NURSE. AM I A NURSE?	THEY WERE ABSENT. THEY WERE NOT ABSENT. WERE THEY ABSENT?	HE WILL BE AN ENGINEER. HE WILL NOT BE AN ENGINEER. WILL HE NOT BE AN ENGINEER?
(+) (-) (?)	WE ARE TEACHERS. WE ARE NOT TEACHERS. ARE WE, TEACHERS?		

FUNCTIONAL GRAMMAR: LESSON -2

TO HAVE (USE OF HAS/ HAVE, HAD, WILL HAVE/SHALL HAVE)

TO DESCRIBE POSSESSION/OWNERSHIP/RELATIONSHIP

When we want to describe possessions, the sentences can be formed by using has/have in the present sense, by using had in the past sense, and by using will have/shall have in the future sense. These types of sentences are also known as non-action sentences, as they have not any main verb.

जब हम संपत्ति का वर्णन करना चाहते हैं, इन प्रकार के वाक्यों को गैर-क्रिया वाक्य के रूप में भी जाना जाता है, क्योंकि उनके पास कोई मुख्य क्रिया नहीं है

Present sense

- Ajay has two cars.

- I have an ink-pen.

- They have a big house.

- He has five pairs of shoes.

- I have two blankets.

- We have three jackets.

Past sense

- Earlier, I had an umbrella.

- We had a beautiful bungalow.

- He had a blue car.

- He had two acres of land.

- They had two cows.

- My friend had a computer.

Future sense

- In the future, I shall have a big farmhouse in Delhi.

The use of different helping verbs:

SUBJECTS	HAS/HAVE	HAD	WILL HAVE/ SHALL HAVE
I	Have	Had	Shall have
We	Have	Had	Shall have
You	Have	Had	Will have
He	Has	Had	Will have
She	Has	Had	Will have
It	Has	Had	Will have
They	Have	Had	Will have
Singular noun	Has	Had	Will have
Plural noun	Have	Had	Will have

We can make negative and interrogative sentences by just adding not with the helping verbs or shifting the helping verbs before the subjects.

	PRESENT HAS/HAVE	PAST HAD	FUTURE WILL HAVE/ SHALL HAVE
(+) (-)	He has a clinic. He has no clinic.	He had a car. He had no car.	I shall have a bicycle. I shall not have a bicycle.
(+) (-)	I have a mobile. I have no mobile.	They had laptops. They had no laptops.	He will have a big house. He will not have a big house.

With the help of this concept we can describe ours' and others' possessions.

For example:

Kavita has a beautiful house.

NOTE: while making negative and interrogative sentences in the present and past senses, we can also use do, does and did to show possessions.

I have no car.	I don't have a car	Do I have a car?
He has no pen.	He doesn't have a car	Does he have a car?
We had no bicycle.	We didn't have a bicycle.	Did we have a bicycle?

FUNCTIONAL GRAMMAR: LESSON -3
(TO DO)

TO DESCRIBE ACTIONS (TENSES)

Present Simple Tense

The Present Simple tense is the most basic in English and uses the base form of the VERB). The only change from the base is the addition of S/ES for the third person singular. This tense is used to describe general habits, commands/orders/requests/possessions.

The base structures for this tense are:

(I, you, we, they and plural nouns)Subject + Verb 1 +object

(He, she, it and singular nouns or name) Subject +Verb 1(s/ es)+object

	Subject	auxiliary verb		main verb	
+	I, you, we, they			like	coffee.
	He, she, it			likes	coffee.
-	I, you, we, they	do	not	like	coffee.
	He, she, it	does	not	like	coffee.
?	Do	I, you, we, they		like	coffee?
	Does	he, she, it		like	coffee?

Present Continuous Tense

This tense is used when the action is progressive, which means, we are doing something.

The base structure for this tense is:

Subject + is/am/are + verb +ing + object

	Subject	auxiliary verb		main verb	
+	I	am		listening	to you.
+	You	are		reading	this.
-	She	is	not	staying	in India.
-	We	are	not	playing	tennis.
?	Is	he		watching	TV?
?	Are	they		waiting	for Paras?

Present Perfect Tense

The Present Perfect tense is rather important in English, as it is used when the action has been completed.

The base structure for this tense is:
Subject + has/have + verb 3rd + object

	Subject	auxiliary verb		main verb	
+	I	have		seen	him.
+	You	have		eaten	my burger.
-	She	has	not	been	to Rome.
-	We	have	not	played	football.
?	Have	you		finished?	
?	Have	they		done	it?

Present Perfect Continuous Tense

This tense is a combination of continuous and perfect action. In our daily lives when we refer to time in progressive action, we can use this tense. The Present Perfect Continuous uses two auxiliary verbs together with the main verb. The use of for and since is done to clarify the time factor in the action. 'Since' is used to refer definite time, and for is used to refer indefinite time.

The base structure for this tense is:
Subject + has been/have been + verb + ing + object + since/for + time

	Subject	auxiliary verb		auxiliary verb	main verb	
+	I	have		been	Waiting for you	for one hour.
+	You	have		been	Talking	too much.
-	It	has	not	been	raining.	since morning.
-	We	have	not	been	Playing	football.
?	Have	you		been	Seeing	her?
?	Have	they		been	Doing	their homework?

Past Simple Tense

We can use several tenses and forms to talk about the past, but the Past Simple tense is the one we use most often, It is used to define our actions in the past, that means what we did in the past. This can be used for general actions of the past, yesterday, last year, last month, or any particular year in the past.

There are two basic structures for the Past Simple tense:

1. Positive sentences

Subject + Verb 2nd +object

2. Negative sentences

Subject+ did not +Verb 1st +object

	Subject	auxiliary verb		main verb	
+	I			went	to school.
	You			worked	very hard.
-	She	did	not	go	with me.
	We	did	not	work	yesterday.
?	Did	you		go	to London?
	Did	they		work	at home?

Past Continuous Tense

We use this tense to say what we were doing at a particular moment in the past.

The base structure for this tense is:

Subject + was/were +Verb + ing + object

	Subject	auxiliary verb		main verb	
+	I	was		watching	television.
+	You	were		working	hard.
-	He, she, it	was	not	helping	mary.
-	We	were	not	joking.	
?	Were	you		being	silly?
?	Were	they		playing	football?

Past Perfect Tense

This tense reveals the past actions which have been completed in the past.

The structure of the Past Perfect tense is:

Subject + had +Verb3rd + object

	Subject	auxiliary verb		main verb	
+	I	had		finished	my work.
+	You	had		stopped	before me.
-	She	had	not	gone	to school.
-	We	had	not	left.	
?	Had	you		arrived?	

Past Perfect Continuous Tense

This tense is a combination of continuous and perfect action in the past. In our daily lives, when we refer to time in progressive action in the past, we can use this tense. The Present Perfect Continuous uses two auxiliary verbs together with the main verb. The use of for and since is done to clarify the time factor in the action. Since is used to refer definite time, and for is used to refer indefinite time.

The base structure for this tense is:
Subject + had been + verb + ing + object + since/for + time

The structure of the Past Perfect Continuous tense is:

	Subject	auxiliary verb		auxiliary verb	main verb	
+	I	had		been	working	for 2 hrs.
+	You	had		been	playing	tennis for 15 minutes.
-	It	had	not	been	working	well for 5 minutes.
-	We	had	not	been	expecting	her since 9'o clock.
?	Had	you		been	drinking	for 15 minutes
?	Had	they		been	waiting	for a long time?

Future Simple Tense

The Future Simple tense involves those actions which are going to be completed in the future:

Subject + will/shall+ verb 1st + object

For negative sentences, we insert not between the helping verb and the main verb.

For question sentences, we place a helping verb before the subject.

Look at these example sentences with the Future Simple tense:

	Subject	Helping verb		main verb	
+	I	will		open	the door.
+	You	will		finish	before me.
-	She	will	not	be	at school tomorrow.
-	We	will	not	leave	yet.
?	Will	you		arrive	on time?
?	Will	they		want	dinner?

Future Continuous Tense

The Future Continuous tense is often used in English as a way to talk about something happening continuously at a given point in the future.

The structure of the Future Continuous tense is:

Subject + will be/shall be+ verb 1st + ing + object

Look at these example sentences with the Future Continuous tense:

	subject	auxiliary verb		auxiliary verb	main verb	object
+	I	will		be	working	at 10 am.
+	You	will		be	lying	on a beach tomorrow.
-	She	will	not	be	using	the car.
-	We	will	not	be	having	dinner at home.
?	Will	you		be	playing	football?
?	Will	they		be	watching	television?

Future Perfect Tense

The Future Perfect tense talks about those actions which will have been perfected or completed in the past.

The structure of the Future Perfect tense is:

Subject + will have/shall have+ verb 3rd + object

Look at these example sentences with the Future Perfect tense:

	subject	auxiliary verb		auxiliary verb	main verb	
+	I	will		have	finished	by 10 am.
+	You	will		have	forgotten	me by then.
-	She	will	not	have	gone	to school.
-	We	will	not	have	left.	
?	Will	you		have	arrived?	

Future Perfect Continuous Tense

The Future Perfect Continuous tense looks at the past from the future about those actions which will have been continuing for some time.

The structure of the Future Perfect Continuous tense is:

Subject + will have/shall have+ verb 3rd + object+ since/for

Look at these example sentences with the Future Perfect Continuous tense:

	subject	auxiliary verb		auxiliary verb	auxiliary verb	main verb	
+	I	will		have	been	working	For four hours.
+	You	will		have	been	traveling	for two days.
-	She	will	not	have	been	using	the car.
-	We	will	not	have	been	waiting	long.

The 12 Verb Tenses - Usage

	Past	Present	Future
Simple	I *ate* pizza yesterday. To indicate a past habit – or an action already completed. Can be used with or without adverbs of time.	I *eat* pizza everyday. To express habits or general truth. To indicate a future event on a designated date as part of a plan or arrangement. With 'mental action' verbs: *like, love, want, need, believe, etc.*	I *will eat* pizza tomorrow. To indicate an action, condition, or circumstance which hasn't taken place yet.
Continuous	I *was eating* pizza when you arrived. To indicate uncompleted action of the past (with or without time reference) To indicate persistent habits of the past (with *always, continuously, forever, etc.*)	I *am eating* pizza right now. To indicate action going on at the time of speaking. To indicate temporary action which may not be happening at the time of speaking. With a habitual action verb, especially to indicate a stubborn habit.	I *will be eating* pizza when you arrive. To indicate what will be going on at some time in the future. To indicate planned future events.
Perfect	I *had eaten* all of the pizza when you arrived. To indicate a completed action of the past that happened before another event took place.	I *have eaten* all of the pizza. To indicate past action which is not defined by a time of occurrence. To indicate an action which started in the past and has continued up until now.	I *will have eaten* all of the pizza by the time you arrive. To indicate an action that will be complete before another event takes place.
Perfect Continuous	I *had been eating* pizza for 2 hours when you arrived. To indicate an action in the past that began before a certain point in the past and continued up until that time.	I *have been eating* pizza for 2 hours. To indicate an action which started at some point in the past and may or may not be complete.	I *will have been eating* pizza for 2 hours when you arrive. To indicate an action that will have happened for some time and will not be complete yet at a certain point in the future.

FUNCTIONAL GRAMMAR: LESSON -4
MODALS

What are modals?

Modals are those auxiliary verbs that are used in sentences to make suggestions, obligations, permissions and probabilities, etc.

मोडल सहायक क्रियाएं हैं जिनका सुझाव, दायित्व, अनुमतियां और संभावनाएं आदि के लिए वाक्यों में उपयोग किया जाता है।

The structures of using modals are:

- **Subject + modal + verb 1ˢᵗ + object**

- **Subject + modal +have+ verb 3ʳᵈ + object**

1. **Subject + modal + verb 1ˢᵗ + object**

MODAL	SUB. + MODAL + VERB 1ˢᵗ + OBJECT			
Can	I	can	speak	English.
Could	I	could	lift	him.
Should	I	should	speak	the truth.
Ought to	I	ought to	respect	my parents.
Must	We	must	respect	the law.
Would	I	would	go	to Delhi.
May	It	may	rain	today.
May	You	may	take	may pen.
Might	I	might	go to	Australia next year.
Has to	He	has to	learn	French daily.
Have to	We	have to	learn	English.
Had to	I	had to	sing	a song.
Will have to	I	will have to	help	him.
Need to	You	need to	learn	grammar.
Used to	He	used to	sleep	in the class.

2. **Subject + modal + have + verb 3ʳᵈ + object**

MODAL	SUBJECT+MODAL+HAVE+VERB3ʳᵈ+ OBJECT			
Could have	He	could	have	helped	me.
Should have	He	should	have	learnt	English.
Must have	He	must	have	gone	to Delhi.
Would have	He	would	have	done	his job.

FUNCTIONAL GRAMMAR: LESSON -5

(ACTIVE/PASSIVE)

Why do we need a passive voice?

using passive voice is less common, the usage of passive voice is quite salient for several reasons; such as it is a part of English language, in certain situations, while communicating, if an object comes first in mind, it becomes necessary to use passive voice e.g. The food was cooked by me.

हालांकि निष्क्रिय आवाज का उपयोग कम आम है, निष्क्रिय आवाज का उपयोग कई कारणों के लिए काफी प्रमुख है; जैसे कि यह अंग्रेजी भाषा का एक हिस्सा है, कुछ स्थितियों में, संप्रेषण करते समय, यदि वस्तु पहले ही मन में आती है, तो निष्क्रिय आवाज का उपयोग करना आवश्यक हो जाता है। उदाहरण के लिए, भोजन मेरे द्वारा पकाया गया था

How do we make passive sentences from active sentences?
Follow these five rules.

- Convert the **subject** of your active sentence into **a new object** of the passive sentence.
- Convert the **object** of your active sentence into **a new subject** of the passive sentence.
- Change **the main verb** into the **third form**(past participle).
- Use **a new helping verb** between **new subject and verb** according to tense.
- Use **a preposition** between the **verb** and the **new object**.

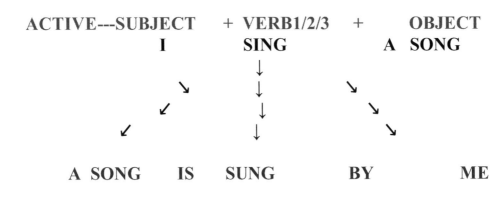

ACTIVE---SUBJECT + VERB1/2/3 + OBJECT
I SING A SONG

A SONG IS SUNG BY ME

PASSIVE----OBJECT + H.V + V3 + PREPOSITION. + SUBJECT
(NEW SUBJECT) (NEW OBJECT)

(Passive helping verbs)

	PRESENT	PAST	FUTURE
INDEFINITE	Is, am& are	Was, were	Will be/shall be
CONTINUOUS	Is being, am being & are being	Was being, were being	No passive
PERFECT	Has been, have been	Had been	Will have been
PERFECT CONTINUOUS	No passive	No passive	No passive

CONVERSION OF SUBJECTS
I→me, we→us, you→you, he→him, she→her, it→it, they→them

Active and Passive Examples

The table below shows example sentences in active and passive voice for the basic tenses as well as various other verb forms, including infinitives and participles.

	Active	Passive
Present Simple	He cooks food.	Food is cooked by him.
Present Continuous	Tushar is helping Tara.	Tushar is being helped by Tushar.
Present Perfect	The kid has served dinner.	Dinner has been served by the kid.
Past Simple	They didn't fix my phone yesterday.	My phone wasn't fixed by them yesterday.
Past Continuous	They were interrogating him	He was being interrogated.
Past Perfect	they hadn't invited me.	I hadn't been invited by them.
Future Simple	They will hang him at dawn.	He will be hanged at dawn by them.
Future Perfect	They will have repaired your car.	Your car will have been repaired by them
Infinitive	I don't want anyone to disturb me.	I don't want to be disturbed by anyone
perfect infinitive	They seem to have taken it.	It seems to have been taken by them.
Participle	I saw the cat eating it.	I saw it being eaten by the cat.
going to	Is he going to sing Thriller at the party?	Is Thriller going to be sung at the party?
used to	He used to take care of everything.	Everything used to be taken care of by him.
Can	They can question him for six hours.	He can be questioned for six hours.
Could	It could have badly hurt you.	You could have been badly hurt by it.
May	The papers say they may release him.	The papers say he may be released.

FUNCTIONAL GRAMMAR: LESSON -6
(SPECIAL STRUCTURES)

To make the English language more profound and comprehensive, we should know a variety of grammar structures that can make us comfortable in rephrasing the sentences.

Practice these structures by making your sentences. Some example sentences have been made for your understanding and convenience.

1. S + FEEL LIKE / LOVE / ENJOY / HATE / ABHOR / + Ving + O   I feel like going for a walk in the morning.   I abhor borrowing the money from the others.
2. I LIKE THE WAY + SENTENCE   I like the way you dance.   I liked the way you cooked food yesterday.
3. S + IS + AM + ARE + ABLE TO + V 1 + O   I am able to convince my friends.   He is able to speak English fluently.
4. S + FIND IT DIFFICULT + TO + V1 + O   I find it difficult to speak English in front of everyone.
5. HELP + S + V1 + O   Help me learn English.   Help me write a letter.(After help we should not use any preposition)
6. S + HAS / HAVE + STARTED / STOPPING + Ving + O   I have stopped smoking.   He has started learning English.
7. S + FIGHT SHY OF + Ving + O   I fight shy of asking her name.   He fights shy of riding a bicycle.
8. S+IS/AM/ARE/WAS / WERE/WILL BE+FOND OF + Ving + O   I am afraid of playing with dogs.   He is afraid of operating machines.
9. S + IS / AM / ARE / WAS / WERE / WILL BE + IN THE HABIT OF + Ving + O   I am in the habit of taking tea in the morning.
10. S + IS + AM + ARE+WAS+ WERE+ADDICTED TO + Ving + O   I am addicted to drinking tea.   Children are addicted to watching television.
11. EARLIER , S + USED TO + V1 + O , BUT NO LONGER NOW   Earlier, I used to smoke cigarettes, but no longer now.
12. S + GET + O + V3 + PREPOSITION + S2   I get my homework done by my brother.

13. BY + Ving + O + SENTENCE   By cooking food, you have won everyone's heart.
14. WHILE + Ving + O + SENTENCE   While driving the car, you should not attend the call.
15. WITHOUT + Ving + O + SENTENCE   Without taking food, you cannot go from here.
16. S + KEEP + Ving + O   I kept sleeping for whole the day.   I keep reading for the whole day.
17. S + INSIST + S2 + ON + Ving + O   He insists me on going to Shimla.
18. S + MAKE + O + ADJECTIVE   That picture made me happy.
19. S + IS / AM / ARE + GETTING + V3   The paper of this book is getting torn.
20. S + IS / AM / ARE + GOOD / BAD AT + Ving + O   I am good at cooking food.   He is bad at playing cricket.
22. S + SHOULD HAVE + V3 + O   He should have helped me.
24. S + IS / AM / ARE + GOING TO + V1 + O   I am going to throw a party.

BASIC GRAMMAR

Learning the basics of any language becomes essential when someone wants to have mastery over the language. Specifically, the students who are appearing for **Duolingo English test** must know the basics of the English language as a certain percentage of grading depends on the actual usage of grammar.

As the whole grammar may be difficult to learn, it is imperative to learn at least the parts of speech, which are important to learn to write and speak correct sentences of the English language. There are eight parts of speech like **1. Noun, 2. Pronoun, 3. Verb, 4. Adverb, 5. Adjective, 6. Preposition, 7. Conjunction, 8. Interjection.** In this book, eight parts of speech and determiners (articles), their usage with examples and worksheets with answers for practice are explained comprehensively and systematically. Students are expected to read this part religiously to get the maximum benefit of this book.

THE PARTS OF SPEECH

The **parts of speech** explain how a word is used in a sentence.

There are eight main parts of speech (also known as word classes): **nouns, pronouns, adjectives, verbs, adverbs, prepositions, conjunctions** and **interjections**.

The eight main parts of speech in English are:

NOUN - (Naming word)

A noun is the name of a person, place, thing or idea.

Examples of nouns: Sam, London, table, dog, teacher, pen, city, happiness, hope

Example sentences: **Steve** lives in **Sydney**. **Mary** uses a **pen** and **paper** to write **letters**.

PRONOUN - (Replaces a Noun)

A pronoun is used in place of a noun or noun phrase to avoid repetition.

Examples of pronouns: I, you, we, they, he, she, it, me, us, them, him, her, this, those

Example sentences: Mary is tired. **She** wants to sleep. **I** want **her** to dance with **me**.

ADJECTIVE - (Describing word)

An **adjective** describes, modifies or gives more information about a noun or pronoun.

Examples: big, happy, green, young, fun, crazy, three

Example sentences: The **little** girl had a **pink** hat.

VERB - (Action Word)

A **verb** shows an action or state of being. A verb shows what someone or something is being done.

Examples: go, speak, run, eat, play, live, walk, have, like, are, is

Example sentences: I **like** the English language. I **study** their charts and **play** their games.

ADVERB - (Describes a verb and adjective)

An **adverb** describes/modifies a verb, an adjective or another adverb. It tells how, where, when, how often or to what extent. Many adverbs end in –LY Examples: slowly, quietly, very, always, never, too, well, tomorrow, here

Example sentences: I am **usually** busy. **Yesterday**, I ate my lunch **quickly**.

PREPOSITION - (Shows relationship)

A **preposition** shows the relationship of a noun or pronoun to another word. They can indicate time, place, or relationship.

Examples: at, on, in, from, with, near, between, about, under

Example sentences: I left my keys **on** the table **for** you.

CONJUNCTION - (Joining word)

A **conjunction** joins two words, ideas, phrases or clauses together in a sentence and shows how they are connected.

Examples: and, or, but, because, so, yet, unless, since, if.

Example sentences: I was hot **and** exhausted **but** I still finished the marathon.

INTERJECTION - (Expressive word)

An **interjection** is a word or phrase that expresses a strong feeling or emotion. It is a short exclamation.

Examples: Ouch! Wow! Great! Help! Oh! Hey! Hi!

Example sentences: Wow! Your shirt is really pretty.

Ouch! that hurts.

BASIC GRAMMAR LESSON-1
NOUN

Definition: The name of a person, place or thing is called a noun.

किसी भी व्यक्ति, स्थान और वस्तु के नाम को संज्ञा कहते है।

Here are some examples:

- person: man, woman, teacher, Ajay, Seema, Ranjan, Satyender

- place: home, office, town, India, city, metro, village

- thing: pen, pencil, banana, music, bed, sheet, love, dog, monkey

Another way of recognizing a noun is by its:

- ending

- position

- function

1. Noun ending

Certain word endings show that a word is a noun, for example:

- -ity → purity

- -ment → management

- -ness → tiredness

- -ation → relation

- -hood → childhood

2. Position in sentence

We can often recognize a noun by its position in the sentence.

Nouns often come after a determiner (a determiner is a word like a, an, the, this, my, such):

- a relief

- an afternoon

- the doctor

- this word

- my house

- such stupidity

3. Function in a sentence

Nouns have certain functions in a sentence, for example:

- the subject of the verb: Doctors work hard.
- an object of the verb: He likes coffee.
- subject and object of the verb: Teachers teach students.

Noun Countability

The major division of English nouns is into "countable" and "uncountable".

Countable Nouns

Countable nouns are easy to recognize. They are things that we can count. For example "pen". We can count pens. We can have one, two, three or more pens. Here are some more countable nouns:

pen, pencil, dog, cat, animal, man, person

Uncountable Nouns

Uncountable nouns are substances, concepts, etc that we cannot divide into separate elements. We cannot "count" them. For example, we cannot count "milk". We can count "bottles of milk" or "liters of milk", but we cannot count "milk" itself. Here are some more uncountable nouns:

music, art, love, happiness, advice, information, news, furniture, luggage, rice, sugar, butter, water, electricity, gas, power, money, currency

We usually treat uncountable nouns as singular. We use a singular verb. For example:

- This news is very important.
- Your luggage looks heavy.

BASIC GRAMMAR LESSON-2
PRONOUN

What is a Pronoun?

Pronoun: a word that takes the place of a noun or represents a noun.

Pronoun: एक शब्द जो एक संज्ञा की जगह लेता है या एक संज्ञा का प्रतिनिधित्व करता है।

Pronouns are small words that take the place of a noun. We can use a pronoun instead of a noun. Pronouns are words like he, you, ours, themselves, some, and each. If we didn't have pronouns, we would have to repeat a lot of nouns.

We would have to say things like:

- Do you like the manager? I don't like the manager. The manager is not friendly.

With pronouns, we can say:

- Do you like the manager? I don't like him. He's not friendly.

In the sentence "Please give this letter to Ajay", we can replace "this letter" with "it" and "Ajay" with "him", as you see below:

| Please give | this letter | To | Ajay. |
| Please give | It | To | him. |

Types of pronouns

Personal Pronouns

Case	Subject		Object		Possessive	
Number	Singular	Plural	Singular	Plural	Singular	Plural
1st Person	I	we	me	us	my, mine	our, ours
2nd Person	you	you	you	you	Your, yours	Your, yours
3rd Person	He, she, it	they	Him, her, it	them	His, her, hers, its	their, theirs

Possessive pronouns

Possessive pronouns are used in English to avoid repeating information that is already clear. In general, it makes the sentence less confusing because the same information is not being repeated.

This book is my book, not your book. (Sounds repetitive)
This book is **mine**, not **yours**. (Mine and yours are **possessive pronouns**)

Examples:

- I didn't have my umbrella, so Mamta lent me **hers**.
  (I didn't have my umbrella, so Mamta lent me her umbrella).

Remember that with possessive pronouns there are no apostrophes (').

Demonstrative Pronouns

We use **this** (singular) and **these** (plural) to refer to something that is **here / near**.

Examples:

- **This** is my pencil. (singular)
- **These** are our children. (plural)

We use **that** (singular) and **those** (plural) to refer to something that is **there / far**.

Examples:

- **That** is our office. (singular)
- **Those** are my shirts. (plural)

Interrogative Pronouns

We use interrogative pronouns to ask questions. The interrogative pronoun represents the thing that we don't know (what we are asking the question about).

There are four main interrogative pronouns: who, whom, what, which

Look at these example questions.

Question	Answer
Who told you?	John told me.
Whom did you tell?	I told Mary.
What has happened?	An accident has happened.

Reflexive Pronouns

Reflexive pronouns reflect on the subject, like a mirror

We use a reflexive pronoun when we want to refer back to the subject of the sentence or clause. Reflexive pronouns end in "-self" (singular) or "-selves" (plural).

There are eight reflexive pronouns:

	reflexive pronoun
Singular	myself yourself himself, herself, itself
Plural	ourselves yourselves themselves.

Look at these examples:

REFLEXIVE pronouns the <u>underlined</u> words are the SAME person/thing
<u>I</u> saw <u>myself</u> in the mirror.
Why do <u>you</u> blame <u>yourself</u>?
<u>Gaurav</u> sent <u>himself</u> a copy.
<u>Rani</u> sent <u>herself</u> a copy.

Reciprocal Pronouns

We use reciprocal pronouns when each of two or more subjects is acting in the same way towards the other. For example, A is talking to B, and B is talking to A. So we say:

- A and B are talking to each other.

There are only two reciprocal pronouns, and they are both two words:

- each other
- one another

Look at these examples:

- Ram and Seeta love each other.
- The ten prisoners were all blaming one another.

Indefinite Pronouns

An indefinite pronoun does not refer to any specific person, thing or amount. It is vague and "not definite". Some typical indefinite pronouns are:

- all, another, any, anybody/anyone, anything, each, everybody/everyone, everything, few, many, nobody, none, one, several, some, somebody/someone

Most indefinite pronouns are either singular or plural. However, some of them can be singular in one context and plural in another. The most common indefinite pronouns are listed below, with examples, as singular, plural or singular/plural.

- Each of the players has a doctor.
- I met two girls. One has given me her phone number.

Relative Pronouns

A relative pronoun is a pronoun that introduces a relative clause. It is called a "relative" pronoun because it "relates" to the word that its relative clause modifies. Here is an example:

- The person who phoned me last night is my teacher.

In the above example, "who": relates to "The person", which "who phoned me last night" modifies

- There are five relative pronouns: who, whom, whose, which, that

BASIC GRAMMAR LESSON-3
ADJECTIVE

What is an Adjective?

An adjective is a word used to describe, point out or specify the number of the person, animal, place or thing specified in a noun. An adjective is used to incorporate additional meaning to any noun - to describe the object.

Types of adjectives

There are 6 types of English adjectives that every student must know.

1. Adjective of Quality

These adjectives add information and qualities to the words they're modifying.

Examples:

"The beautiful flowers have a nice smell" gives us a lot more information with two qualitative adjectives.

You can say "The dog is hungry," or "The hungry dog." In both cases, the word hungry is an adjective describing the dog. I have a blue shirt.

2.Adjective of Quantity

Describe the quantity of something.

In other words, they answer the question "how much?" or "how many?" Numbers like one and thirty are this type of adjective. So are more general words like many, half and a lot.

Examples:

"How many children do you have?" "I only have one son."

"Do you plan on having more kids?" " yes, I want many kids playing around me."

"I can't believe I ate that whole pastry!"

3. Demonstrative

A **demonstrative adjective** describes "which" noun or pronoun you're referring to. These adjectives include the words:

- **This** — Used to refer to a singular noun close to you. "This pen is mine."
- **That** — Used to refer to a singular noun far from you. "That pen is yours."
- **These** — Used to refer to a plural noun close to you. "These shirts are mine."
- **Those** — Used to refer to a plural noun far from you."Those shirts are yours."

4. Possessive

Possessive adjectives show possession. They describe to whom a thing belongs. Some of the most common possessive adjectives include:

- **My** — Belonging to me
- **His** — Belonging to him
- **Her** — Belonging to her
- **Their** —Belonging to them
- **Your** —Belonging to you
- **Our** — Belonging to us

All these adjectives, except the word his, can only be used before a noun. You can't just say "That's my," you have to say "That's my pen." When you want to leave off the noun or pronoun being modified, use these possessive adjectives instead:

- **Mine**
- **His**
- **Hers**
- **Theirs**
- **Yours**
- **Ours**

For example, even though saying "That's my" is incorrect, saying "That's mine" is fine.

Examples:
"Whose cat is that?" "That's mine. That's my cat."

5. Interrogative

Interrogative adjectives interrogate, meaning that they ask a question. These adjectives are always followed by a noun or a pronoun and are used to form questions. The interrogative adjectives are:

- **Which** — Asks to choose between options.
- **What** — Asks to make a choice (in general).
- **Whose** — Asks who something belongs to.

Other question words, like "who" or "how," aren't adjectives since they don't modify nouns. For example, you can say "Whose coat is this?" but you can't say "who coat?"

Which, what and whose are only considered adjectives if they're immediately followed by a noun. The word which is an adjective in this sentence: "Which pen is your favorite?" But not in this one: "Which is your favorite pen?"

Examples:

"Which song will you play on your wedding day?"

"What pet do you want to get?"

"Whose dog is this?"

6. Distributive

Distributive adjectives describe specific members out of a group. These adjectives are used to single out one or more individual items or people. Some of the most common distributive adjectives include:

Each — Every single one of a group (used to speak about group members individually).

Every — Every single one of a group (used to make generalizations).

Either — One between a choice of two.

Neither — Not one or the other between a choice of two.

Any — One or some things out of any number of choices. This is also used when the choice is irrelevant, like: "it doesn't matter, I'll take *any* of them."

These adjectives are always followed by the noun or pronoun they're modifying.

Examples:

"Every dog has its day ."

"Which of these two pens do you like?" "I don't like either song."

3 DIFFERENT DEGREES OF ADJECTIVES

The three degrees of an adjective
are **positive**, **comparative** and **superlative**. When you use them
depends on how many things you're talking about:

- **A positive adjective** is a normal adjective that's used to describe, not compare. For example: "This is good juice" and "I am not a funny *boy.*"
- **A comparative adjective** is an adjective that is used to compare two things (and is often followed by the word than*)*. For example: "This coffee is bette*r* than that tea", or "I am funnie*r* than her."
- **A superlative adjective** is an adjective that's used to compare three or more things, or to state that something is the most. For example: "You are the *best* father in the whole world" or "I am the richest out of all the other bloggers."

These three degrees only work for **qualitative** adjectives.

Adjective Order

There are 2 basic positions for adjectives:

1. Before the noun and
2. After some verbs (be, become, get, seem, look, feel, sound, smell, taste)

Adjective Before Noun

We often use more than one adjective before the noun:

I like big black dogs.

She was wearing a beautiful long red dress.

Adjective After Verb

An adjective can come after some verbs, such as: *be, become, feel, get, look, seem, smell, sound*

Even when an adjective comes after the verb and not before a noun, it always refers to and qualifies the subject of the clause, not the verb.

Look at the examples below: subject-verb adjective

- Ram is Indian.
- Is it getting dark?
- The examination did not seem difficult.

BASIC GRAMMAR LESSON-4
VERB

What is a verb:

A verb is one of the main parts of a sentence or question in English and has got the status of an important part of speech. One can't think of a sentence or a question without a verb.

एक क्रिया अंग्रेजी में एक वाक्य या प्रश्न के मुख्य भागों में से एक है, और भाषण के एक महत्वपूर्ण हिस्से का दर्जा प्राप्त किया है। वास्तव में, कोई क्रिया के बिना किसी वाक्य या प्रश्न का विचार नहीं कर सकता है।

Types of verbs

Action verbs

Action verbs express specific actions, and are used any time you want to show action or discuss someone doing something.

e.g.-He always plays football in the afternoon.

Transitive verbs

These verbs always have direct objects, meaning someone or something receives the action of the verb.

e.g.-He goes to market.

Intransitive Verbs
No direct object follows an intransitive verb.

e.g.-He laughs.

Auxiliary verbs

Auxiliary verbs are also known as helping verbs, and are used together with a main verb to show the verb's tense or to form a question or negative.

e.g.-He is playing the role of my partner.

Stative verbs

Stative verbs can be recognized because they express a state rather than an action. They typically relate to thoughts, emotions, relationships, senses, states of being, and measurements. e.g.

I am feeling sad.

Modal verbs

Modal verbs are auxiliary verbs that are used to express abilities, possibilities, permissions, and obligations.

e.g.-He can speak French.

Phrasal verbs

Phrasal verbs aren't single words; instead, they are combinations of words that are used together to take on a different meaning to that of the original verb.

e.g.-He has put on weight.

BASIC GRAMMAR LESSON-5
ADVERB

Adverbs:

Adverbs are used to modify verbs. Adverbs can also be used to modify adjectives and other adverbs. Adverbs are an important part of speech. They usually answer questions such as how? where? when? how often? and how much?

क्रियाविशेषण क्रियाओं को संशोधित करने के लिए उपयोग किया जाता है क्रियाविशेषण का उपयोग विशेषण और अन्य क्रियाविशेषण को संशोधित करने के लिए भी किया जा सकता है। क्रियाविशेषण भाषण का एक महत्वपूर्ण अंग हैं वे आम तौर पर ऐसे सवालों के जवाब देते हैं जैसे कि कैसे? कहा पे? कब? कितनी बार? और कितना?

Kinds of Adverbs

Adverbs of Manner

Adverbs of Manner tell us the manner or way in which something happens. They answer the question "how?". Adverbs of Manner mainly modify verbs.

- He speaks slowly. (How does he speak?)
- They helped us cheerfully. (How did they help us?)
- James Bond drives his cars fast. (How does James Bond drive his cars?)

Adverbs of Place

Adverbs of Place tell us the place where something happens. They answer the question "where?" Adverbs of Place mainly modify verbs.

- Please sit here. (Where should I sit?)
- They looked everywhere. (Where did they look?)

Adverbs of Time

Adverbs of Time tell us something about the time that something happens. Adverbs of Time mainly modify verbs.

They can answer the question "when?":

- He came yesterday. (When did he come?)
- I want it now. (When do I want it?)

Or they can answer the question "how often?" (frequency):

- They deliver the newspaper daily. (How often do they deliver the newspaper?)

- We sometimes watch a movie. (How often do we watch a movie?)

Adverbs of Degree

Adverbs of Degree tell us the degree or extent to which something happens. They answer the question "how much?" or "to what degree? Adverbs of Degree can modify verbs, adjectives and other adverbs.

- She entirely agrees with him. (How much does she agree with him?)
- Mary is very beautiful. (To what degree is Mary beautiful? How beautiful is Mary?)

Adverb Position

When an adverb modifies a verb, there are usually 3 possible positions within the sentence or clause:

1. FRONT - before the subject		Now	I will read a book.
2. MID - between subject + verb	I	Often	Read books.

When an adverb modifies an adjective or another adverb, it usually goes in front of the word that it modifies, for example:

	Adverb	Adjective	
She gave him a	Really	Dirty	look.
	Adverb	Adverb	
We	Quite	Often	study English.

The position of an adverb often depends on the kind of adverb (manner, place, time, degree).

BASIC GRAMMAR LESSON-6
ARTICLES

The determiners a/an and they are called "articles". They are the most common of all determiners. They come at the very beginning of a noun phrase. We divide them into "indefinite" and "definite" like this:

निर्धारितकर्ताओं ए / एक को "लेख" कहा जाता है वे एक संज्ञा/वाक्यांश की बहुत शुरुआत में आते हैं। हम उन्हें "अनिश्चित" और "निश्चित" इस तरह विभाजित करते हैं:

	Indefinite articles	Definite article
	a/an	The
Used with	singular countable nouns only	all nouns
used for	a non-specific person or thing (singular)	specific people or things (singular or plural)

Think of the sky at night. In the sky, we see MILLIONS of stars and ONE moon. So normally we would say:

- I saw *a* star last night.

- I saw *the* moon last night.

Look at some more examples:

a/an	The
I was born in a town. Rohit had an omelet for lunch. Tushar ordered a cold drink. We want to buy an umbrella. Have you got a pen?	The capital of India is not Paris. I have found the book that I lost. Have you cleaned the car? There are six eggs in the fridge. Please switch off the TV when you finish.

Of course, often we can use a/an or the for the same word. It depends on the situation, not the word. Look at these examples:

- We want to buy an umbrella. (Any umbrella, not a particular umbrella.)

- It's raining! Where is the umbrella? (We already have an umbrella. We are looking for our umbrella, a particular umbrella.)

Articles with Countable and Uncountable Nouns

Notice that we use the indefinite article a/an ONLY with singular countable nouns: a dog, an egg, a very big man, an extremely delicious meal

By contrast, we can use the definite article 'the' with ALL nouns: the dog, the eggs, the big men, the music, the food, the red wine

It is sometimes also possible to have no article at all—the so-called ZERO article. This can happen with all nouns (but normally not singular countable nouns): dogs, eggs, hot meals, music, red wine

The following table shows how we usually use articles with countable and uncountable nouns.

		a/an	The	ZERO
Countable	Singular	a dog	the dog	~~dog~~
	Plural	~~a dogs~~	the dogs	dogs
Uncountable		~~a music~~	the music	music

In English, a singular countable noun usually needs an article (or another determiner) in front of it. We cannot say: ~~I saw elephant yesterday.~~

We need to say something like:

- I saw an elephant.
- I saw a pink elephant.
- I saw the elephant.
- I saw your elephant.

BASIC GRAMMAR LESSON-7
PREPOSITION

Preposition: a part-of-speech usually coming before a noun phrase and connecting it to another part of the sentence

The name preposition (pre + position) means "PLACE BEFORE". A preposition typically comes BEFORE another word—usually a noun phrase. It tells us about the relationship between the noun phrase and another part of the sentence. Some very common prepositions are: in, of, on, for, with, at, by.

हमें संज्ञा और वाक्य के दूसरे भाग के बीच संबंध के बारे में बताता है। कुछ बहुत ही आम व्याख्याएं हैं: में, के, पर, के लिए, के साथ, पर, द्वारा

PREPOSITIONS - TIME

English	Usage	Example
On	days of the week	on Monday
in	months / seasons time of day year after a certain period (when?)	in August / in winter in the morning in 2006 in an hour
at	for night for a weekend a certain point of time (when?)	at night at the weekend at half-past nine
since	from a certain point of time (past till now)	since 1980
for	over a certain period (past till now)	for 2 years
ago	a certain time in the past	2 years ago
Before	earlier than a certain point of time	before 2004
to	telling the time	ten to six (5:50)
past	telling the time	ten past six

English	Usage	Example
		(6:10)
to / till	marking the beginning and end of a period	from Monday to/till Friday
till / until	in the sense of how long something is going to last	He is on holiday until Friday.
By	in the sense of at the latest up to a certain time	I will be back by 6 o'clock. By 11 o'clock, I had read five pages.

PREPOSITIONS - LOCATION

In	room, building, street, town, country book, paper, etc. car, taxi picture, world	in the kitchen, in London in the book in the car, in a taxi in the picture, in the world
at	meaning next to, by an object for table for events a place where you are to do something typical (watch a film, study, work)	at the door, at the station at the table at a concert, at the party at the cinema, at school, at work

on	attached	the picture on the wall
	for a place with a river	London lies on the Thames.
	being on a surface	on the table
	for a certain side (left, right)	on the left
	for a floor in a house	on the first floor
	for public transport	on the bus, on a plane
	for television, radio	
by, next to, beside	left or right of somebody or something	Jane is standing by / next to/beside the car.
Under	on the ground, lower than (or covered by) something else	the bag is under the table
below	lower than something else but above ground	the fish are below the surface
over	covered by something else	put a jacket over your shirt
	meaning more than	over 16 years of age
	getting to the other side (also across)	walk over the bridge
	overcoming an obstacle	climb over the wall
above	higher than something else, but not directly over it	a path above the lake

across	getting to the other side (also over) getting to the other side	walk across the bridge swim across the lake
through	something with limits on top, bottom and the sides	drive through the tunnel
to	a movement to person or building a movement to a place or country for bed	go to the cinema go to London / Ireland go to bed
into	enter a room / a building	go into the kitchen / the house
towards	movement in the direction of something (but not directly to it)	go 5 steps towards the house
onto	a movement to the top of something	jump onto the table
from	in the sense of where from	a flower from the garden

PREPOSITIONS - GENERAL

English	Usage	Example
from	who gave it	a present from Jack
of	who/what does it belong to what does it show	a page of the book the picture of a palace
by	who made it	a book by Mark Twain
on	walking or riding on horseback entering a public transport vehicle	on foot, on horseback get on the bus
in	entering a car / Taxi	get in the car
off	leaving a public transport vehicle	get off the train
out of	leaving a car / Taxi	get out of the taxi
by	rise or fall of something traveling (other than walking or horse-riding)	prices have risen by 10 percent by car, by bus
at	for *age*	she learned Russian at 45
about	for topics, meaning *what about*	we were talking about you

BASIC GRAMMAR LESSON-8
CONJUNCTION

The Conjunction is a word that joins together words, phrases and clauses.

संयोजन एक शब्द है जो शब्दों, वाक्यांशों और धाराओं को जोड़ता है

A conjunction is a word that connects two parts of a sentence.

संयोजन एक शब्द है जो वाक्य के दो हिस्सों को जोड़ता है

- bread and butter (joins two words)
- up the stairs and along the corridor (joins two phrases)
- Ajay likes tea and Akhil likes coffee (joins two clauses)

Here are some other common conjunctions:

and, but, or, nor, for, yet, so, although, because, since, unless

Types of Conjunctions

Coordinating conjunctions are used to join two parts of a sentence that are grammatically equal. The two parts may be single words or clauses, for example:

Ram and Sham went up the hill.

I worked hard, but I failed.

Subordinating conjunctions are used to join a subordinate dependent clause to the main clause, for example:

I did not come to your office because I was ill.

Correlative Conjunctions correlate work in pairs to join phrases or words that carry equal importance within a sentence. For example:

She is both intelligent and beautiful.

Coordinating Conjunctions

A coordinating conjunction joins parts of a sentence (for example words or independent clauses) that are grammatically equal or similar. Coordinating conjunction shows that the elements it joins are similar in importance and structure: There are seven coordinating conjunctions, and they are all short words of only two or three letters:

- and, but, or, nor, for, yet, so

Look at these examples - the two elements that the coordinating conjunction joins are shown in square brackets [ ]:

- I like **[tea]** and **[coffee]**.

- **[Ram likes tea]**, but **[Sham likes coffee]**.

Coordinating conjunctions always come between the words or clauses that they join.

When a coordinating conjunction joins independent clauses, it is always correct to place a comma before the conjunction:

- I want to work as an interpreter in the future, so I am studying Spanish at university.

However, if the independent clauses are short and well-balanced, a comma is not essential:

- She is kind so she helps people.

The 7 coordinating conjunctions are short, simple words. They have only two or three letters. There's an easy way to remember them - their initials spell "FANBOYS", like this:

F	A	N	B	O	Y	S
For	And	Nor	But	or	Yet	So

Subordinating Conjunctions

A subordinating conjunction is used to link a <u>subordinate clause</u> (also known as a <u>dependent clause</u>) to the main clause (also known as an <u>independent clause</u>).

In each example below, the main clause is in bold, and the subordinating conjunction is shaded.

- She left early because Ashok arrived with his new girlfriend.
- Keep your hand on the wound until the doctor asks you to take it off.

The Function of a Subordinating Conjunction

The subordinating conjunction provides the bridge between the main clause and the dependent clause.

Subordinating conjunctions and commas

When a subordinate clause starts a sentence, it is normal to separate it from the main clause with a comma. For example:

If you answer my question, I will give you a prize.

When a subordinate clause ends a sentence, you should drop the comma.

I will not help him if he does not come to me.

Correlative Conjunctions

Correlative conjunctions are fun to use. At the same time, there are some important rules to remember.

- When using correlative conjunctions, ensure verbs agree, so your sentences make sense.

  For example: Every night, **either** you **or** your friends **wake** Sonia from her sleep.

- When you use correlative conjunction, you must be sure that the pronoun agrees.

  For example: **Neither** Ashok **nor** Seema expressed **her** annoyance when Ranjan broke the glass.

- When using correlative conjunctions, be sure to keep the parallel structure intact. Equal grammatical units need to be incorporated into the entire sentence.

  For example, He not only **came** to my house but also **took** the food.

Other examples of Correlative Conjunctions

He **neither** attends his office **nor** submits his resignation.

You can **either** watch TV **or** play video games.

Whether you have taken your meal **or** not?

He is **too** poor **to** donate.

He is **so** poor **that** he cannot donate.

Whether rich **or** poor, everyone has to die one day.

He **not only** patted my back **but also** gave me a prize.

BASIC GRAMMAR LESSON-9
INTERJECTION

What is an interjection?

An interjection is a word that expresses some kind of emotion. It can be used as a filler. Interjections do not have a grammatical function in the sentence and are not related to the other parts of the sentence. If an interjection is omitted, the sentence still makes sense. It can stand alone.

विस्मयादिबोध एक शब्द है जो किसी प्रकार की भावना व्यक्त करता है। यह भराव के रूप में इस्तेमाल किया जा सकता है इंटरजेक्शन के वाक्य में एक व्याकरण समारोह नहीं है और वाक्य के दूसरे भागों से संबंधित नहीं हैं। यदि कोई विराम छोड़ दिया जाता है, तो वाक्य अभी भी समझ में आता है। यह अकेले खड़े हो सकते हैं

- Ouch! That hurts.
- Well, I need a break.

When you are expressing a strong emotion, use an exclamation mark (!). A comma (,) can be used for a weaker emotion.

Kinds of Interjections

1. Expressing a feeling—wow, oops, oh:

- Oops, I'm sorry. That was my mistake.
- Oh, I didn't know that.
- Wow! What a beautiful dress!

2. Saying yes or no—yes, no, nope:

- Yes! I will do it!
- No, I am not going to go there.
- Nope. That's not what I want.

3. Calling attention—yo, hey:

- Yo, will you throw the ball back?
- Hey, I just wanted to talk to you about the previous incident.

4. Indicating a pause—well, um, hmm:

- Well, what I meant was nothing like that.
- Um, here is our proposal.

FINAL TIP FOR PASSING WITH THE FLYING COLOURS

This exam has been designed to test your general level of English and is not based on specific exam techniques needed for tests like PTE, IELTS or TOEFL.

The best way to prepare for this is to improve your general language by taking classes with a teacher or doing some self-study. Although we always recommend students to study themselves, we think the most effective way for a student to improve is by combining this with taking lessons from a qualified English teacher.

Preparing for any kind of test can be an uphill task but at English World, we're here to help you. If you're interested in doing some preparation for the Duolingo test, get in touch with our experienced and qualified teachers who can help you achieve your goal.

For all Inquiries please contact at helpline 9416821236 (from 9 AM to 5 PM), or drop a mail at **englishworldkurukshetra@gmail.com**

Made in the USA
Columbia, SC
20 October 2020